The Care and Education of a Deaf Child

PARENTS' and TEACHERS' GUIDES

Series Editor
Professor Colin Baker, *University of Wales, Bangor, Wales, UK.*

Dyslexia: A Parents' and Teachers' Guide
    TREVOR PAYNE and ELIZABETH TURNER
A Parents' and Teachers' Guide to Bilingualism
    COLIN BAKER
Second Language Students in Mainstream Classrooms
    COREEN SEARS

Other Books of Interest
Building Bridges: Multilingual Resources for Children
    MULTILINGUAL RESOURCES FOR CHILDREN PROJECT
Child-Rearing in Ethnic Minorities
    J.S. DOSANJH and PAUL A.S. GHUMAN
Japanese Children Abroad: Cultural, Educational and Language Issues
    ASAKO YAMADA-YAMAMOTO and BRIAN RICHARDS (eds)
Multicultural Children in the Early Years
    P. WOODS, M. BOYLE and N. HUBBARD
Multicultural Child Care
    P. VEDDER, E. BOUWER and T. PELS
Working with Bilingual Children
    M.K. VERMA, K.P. CORRIGAN and S. FIRTH (eds)
Young Bilingual Children in Nursery Schools
    LINDA THOMPSON

Please contact us for the latest book information:
Multilingual Matters, Frankfurt Lodge, Clevedon Hall,
Victoria Road, Clevedon, BS21 7HH, England
http://www.multilingual-matters.com

PARENTS' AND TEACHERS' GUIDES 4
Series Editor: Colin Baker

The Care and Education of a Deaf Child

A Book for Parents

Pamela Knight and Ruth Swanwick

MULTILINGUAL MATTERS LTD
Clevedon • Buffalo • Toronto • Sydney

Library of Congress Cataloging in Publication Data
Knight, Pamela
The Care and Education of a Deaf Child: A Book for Parents/Pamela Knight and
Ruth Swanwick
Parents' and Teachers Guides: 4
Includes bibliographical references and index
1. Deaf children–Great Britain. 2. Deaf children–Great Britain–Language.
3. Deaf children–Education–Great Britain.
I. Swanwick, Ruth. II Title. III. Series: Parents' and Teachers' Guides: No. 4
HV2716.K65   1999
649'.1512–dc21   99-16169

British Library Cataloguing in Publication Data
A CIP catalogue record for this book is available from the British Library.

ISBN 1-85359-459-8 (hbk)
ISBN 1-85359-458-X (pbk)

Multilingual Matters Ltd
UK: Frankfurt Lodge, Clevedon Hall, Victoria Road, Clevedon BS21 7HH.
USA: UTP, 2250 Military Road, Tonawanda, NY 14150, USA.
Canada: UTP, 5201 Dufferin Street, North York, Ontario M3H 5T8, Canada.
Australia: P.O. Box 586, Artarmon, NSW, Australia.

Typeset by Archetype-IT Ltd (http://www.archetype-it.com).
Printed and bound in Great Britain by The Cromwell Press Ltd.

Contents

Foreword

We are often asked to write a chapter for a book, a section of an article or a module for a course on the bilingual deaf child, bilingualism and deafness, bilingual education and lately it has been sign bilingualism. We have resisted this as we feel strongly that the issue of bilingualism and deaf children is not a bolt-on additional chapter or module to the education of deaf children. We see it as a fundamental concept that has implications across the whole range of deaf issues including a child's degree of deafness, deaf children's language development, cognitive development and educational placement. It affects the policy and practice of delivering an appropriate education for all deaf children.

A sign bilingual approach focuses primarily upon the language and learning needs of the deaf child, regardless of their degree of deafness. We consider that a well developed, sign bilingual approach is able to incorporate the varying needs of all deaf children. This is the central message of this book and we have welcomed the opportunity to write a book for parents where these ideas can be more fully explored.

About the Authors

Pamela Knight is a teacher of deaf children with wide experience of working with deaf children. She has worked in a school for deaf with children from both primary and secondary departments. She has also worked as a teacher supporting deaf children in mainstream schools. The greater part of her work (and enthusiasm) has been with the families of young deaf children and with their early experiences in school.

Ruth Swanwick is also a teacher of deaf children where the greater part of her experience has been working with sign bilingual deaf children in mainstream primary school. Her interest in bilingualism has sprung directly from her background in modern foreign language teaching.

Currently they are both lecturers in deaf education at the School of Education at Leeds University. There they are involved in teacher education both in training teachers of the deaf and also with those studying for higher degrees in deaf education.

Pamela's particular research interests are in bilingual support to

families and the early years education of deaf children, the development
of policy and practice of deaf education and audiology for bilingual deaf
children. Ruth's special areas of interest are the nature of sign bilingualism
and the learning needs of sign bilingual deaf children, particularly literacy
and the development of English as a second language. They have both
published in these areas.

These interests and accumulated experiences of working in deaf
education are reflected in this book. Much of the text has been inspired by
the parents and teachers that they have worked with over the years whose
insights, ideas and enthusiasm are essential ingredients in this exciting
developing area.

Introduction

We were motivated to write this book as a response to the many requests we had to write a chapter for a book, give a talk to parent groups or to give a paper at a conference on bilingualism and deaf children. We were not happy with the idea that there is a lot to know about deafness and deaf children and bilingualism is but one part. We feel strongly that it should be viewed as an integral part of all aspects of deafness and deaf education. How were we to address this problem?

As the parents and families of deaf children are the most important people in their lives we decided to expound our ideas — that bilingualism is not an add-on extra or yet another option — in a book for parents (and for those professionals who work with them).

This posed quite a challenge for us. We have written an introductory book with families who are 'new' to deafness in mind as well as those who are some way down the track, and want to read further about deafness. This means we have focused on the broad issues related to deafness such as language choice and development which are relevant to everyone, as well as some quite specific information about, for example, hearing loss, schools and support systems.

We have focused on what are the issues for the deaf children, their families, their teachers and their friends and emphasised that they all have very special and individual needs. Our belief is in the importance of understanding and establishing what those needs are and meeting them in response to the wishes of the children and the family.

The different chapters in the book address the range of practical and theoretical issues explored. Some chapters are more informative and practical while others attempt to explain the more problematical nature of some of the issues. In this way the practical ideas and suggestions and strategies are supported by theoretical argument.

For many parents, the first thing they want to know is what does deafness mean in practical terms; What caused it? Will it get better? Can it be cured? In response to this need the first section of the book gives a basic overview of medical aspects of hearing loss, what has caused it, how it is measured and an introduction to hearing aids. We then go on to explore deafness in terms of 'models'. One is certainly the 'medical model' with its hospital connotations which are important and need to be addressed. But another way of looking at deafness is in terms of the language issues to be considered as a result of the hearing loss. This is often called a 'linguistic model' of deafness.

This model of deafness really defines the philosophy of the whole book and the standpoint from which the deaf child is viewed; that is while valuing the medical aspects of deafness, the focus subsequently is on the linguistic profile of deaf children.

The second section of the book focuses on the young deaf child and the family at home and the large issue for them of decisions about communication at home and with the family. It also explores the fact that there are likely to be many different people and professionals visiting the family and some of the pressures this fact may bring.

There is a section devoted to deaf children and the use of sign language explaining the ideas that support the use of two languages and then the implications for deaf children who develop sign language skills.

The last section looks more specifically at deaf children and their education. First of all it explains some of the choices that parents will have to make when their child goes to school and then looks at aspects of education, particularly how deaf children may learn to read and to write.

The conclusion to the book is an overview of the issues raised within the bulk of the book and also looks towards the future for deaf education.

Each chapter of the book is complete in itself and so the book may be dipped into depending upon a specific interest of the moment. Over all we hope the book will be informative and as useful to parents and professionals as it has been to us in formulating our ideas in a way that is accessible to those who wish to read more about the lives of deaf children.

Glossary of Terms

We have tried to avoid jargon in this book, as far as is possible, but there is some unavoidable terminology and also in a growing and developing area there are always new words to encounter. We hope that this glossary will help you as you meet unfamiliar terms throughout the book.

Acquired deafness — forms of deafness that have been acquired through trauma or infection such as otitis media or tumours.

Audiogram — is the form on which a hearing loss is recorded. It is unique to each child.

Audiological descriptors — standard terminology used to describe degrees of deafness from guidelines set by the national executive council of the British association of teachers of the deaf.

Audiology — the study of all aspects of hearing and hearing loss.

Auditory world — this term is used to describe a hearing persons access to the environment which includes access to all auditory stimulus.

Bicultural — describes an individual who interacts with two or more cultures in their everyday lives.

Bilingual — describes an individual who uses two or more languages in their everyday lives.

Bottom-up — approaches to getting meaning from text which focus on decoding individual words and letters.

British Sign Language (BSL) — the natural language of the adult deaf community in Great Britain .

Cochlear implant — a cochlear implant is a device implanted into the cochlear which aims to stimulate the auditory nerve directly, to give a sensation of hearing in those unable to benefit from conventional hearing aids.

Cohesive links — the grammatical conventions of a written language which carry an idea through a text such as reference words (e.g. he, she, it, those, these, that) or conjunctions (e.g. and, like, although, if, however).

Conductive deafness — hearing loss associated with problems in the outer and/or middle ear.

Congenital deafness — this largely refers to deafness which is inherited or due to environmental factors such as illness during pregnancy.

Contact signing — communication which include the use of BSL (or ASL) and English which is the result of interaction between deaf and hearing people.

Contrastive analysis — exploration of the properties of a language through contrast and comparison with another language.

Cueing systems — the sources of information about language that a reader uses to get at the meaning of text.

Deaf culture — the shared and historically transmitted experiences, traditions, language, values and aspirations which identify deaf people as a unique group.

Deaf community — the national and local network of deaf people who work for and support the cultural and political interests of deaf people.

Deficit model — a view of deafness which centres on the disabling effects of hearing impairment in the context of the hearing world.

Dominant language/primary language — the language in which high levels of linguistic competence are most easily acquired and through which the individual can most successfully learn.

Early intervention — the support given to families of deaf children from the moment their deafness is diagnosed.

Finger-spelling — a manual representation of each letter of alphabet, which is a feature of sign language use and also a tool for manually representing English.

First language — a child's first language is normally the language of their home environment and of the wider society in which s/he lives.

Function words — words which carry grammatical meaning such as conjunctions, prepositions and articles.

Glue ear — a common condition in young children which affects the middle ear.

Graphophonics — the relationship between letters of the alphabet and their sounds.

Hearing status — this term is used when considering a person or family in terms of whether they are a hearing family a deaf family or a family with both deaf and hearing members.

Interactive — a model of the reading process which synthesises both bottom-up and top-down skills.

Language mixing — the combining of the features of two languages within the same phrase or utterance.

Language switching — the alternate use of two languages within the same utterance.

Linguistic minority — a group of people who share a first language and a culture which is different from that of the society in which they live, with lower status and power.

Learning characteristics — the areas of an individual's learning strengths and weaknesses, sometimes also referred to as **learning styles.**

Lexicon — a speaker's mental dictionary of a particular language.

Linguistic majority — a group of people whose first language is that which is officially recognised and used as the primary language of that society.

Manually coded English — this term describes any form of sign system which supports the use of spoken English.

Manual communication — an umbrella term which refers to communication which involves the use of the hands, this can imply the use of natural sign language or of a manually coded form of English.

Metalinguistic awareness — an ability to reflect upon language as a system.

Mild hearing loss — a hearing loss of between 20–40 dB.

Modality — the medium through which language is expressed (oral/aural, visual/gestural or text).

Moderate hearing loss — a hearing loss of between 41–70 dB.

National Literacy Strategy — a UK government strategy introduced in 1997 to raise standards of literacy in English primary schools which includes national targets and a framework for teaching literacy skills.

Oral method — the method of developing language in deaf children which precludes the use of any form of formalised signs.

Oral/aural communication — the use of the vocal and auditory tract respectively for receptive and expressive communication.

Otitis media – a condition of the middle ear which leads to glue ear.

Phonology — the sound system of a language.

Phonological awareness — an understanding of the patterns and rules for the combination and pronunciation of the sounds of a particular language.

Preferred language — this term is used to describe the language a child would most easily acquire and develop to a level most appropriate to his/her age and development.

Pre-lingual deafness — deafness that has been apparent before a person has begun to develop a language.

Post-lingual deafness — deafness that has been acquired after the person has partially or fully developed their spoken language.

Profound hearing loss — a hearing loss greater than 95 dB.

Recruitment — the sensation of abnormal loudness growth often associated with sensori-neural hearing loss.

Semantics — the linguistic meaning of words and sentences.

Sensori-neural — hearing loss associated with the inner ear and nerve of hearing.

Sequential bilingualism — the acquisition of two languages were one language is introduced and learned after the other.

Severe hearing loss — a hearing loss of between 71–95 dB.

Sign language — the visual/gestural language of the deaf community. In the UK this language is British Sign Language; in the USA it is American Sign Language. Each country develops their own form of sign language.

Sign supported systems/sign supported English — vocabulary of sign language used to support spoken English. the signs are used in the order of the spoken language.

Sign bilingual — describes an individual who engages with sign language and English.

Sign Supported English (SSE) — the use of signs (usually content words) borrowed from BSL to support the spoken form of English.

Simultaneous bilingualism — the acquisition of two languages at the same time.

Syntax — the structure of the phrases and sentences of a language.

Top-down — approaches to meaning from text which focus on the use of contextual and background information.

Total communication — an over-arching term which denotes an approach to the education of deaf children where all modes of communication are considered (confusion arises over the use of this term where it is used to mean the use of simultaneous sign and speech).

Visual/gestural communication — the use of vision and of the movement of the hands, head and body respectively for receptive and expressive communication.

Visual world — a term used to describe a deaf person's view of the world where they have very little access to the sounds of the environment and most particularly of speech.

Part 1

An Introduction to Deafness

Deafness is a fact of life. Deaf people lead lives that are in some ways different, but not inferior to the lives of people with normal hearing.

Freeman *et al.* (1981: 16)

Chapter 1

What it Means to be Deaf

Introduction

You are probably reading this book because you are the parent of a deaf child or are working with deaf children. This first chapter will look at some of the very practical aspects of deafness and is intended to address many of the initial questions about what hearing loss actually means; how hearing works and what can go wrong. This is probably your first encounter with deafness and naturally you will want to understand what deafness means and what may be the causes of deafness in your child. Then there is some explanation about the hearing (audiometric) tests which diagnose and then define the degree of deafness present followed by a description of some of the types of hearing aids available.

The first section will give a basic overview of the mechanism of hearing and subsequently, hearing loss. Causes of deafness are also explored but it is important to appreciate that in many cases the cause cannot be found. Also if the cause is established it does not follow that a cure can be found. Nevertheless it is always interesting to find out as much as you can. There is a description of the type of testing used to diagnose deafness in the first instance and subsequently to find the degree of deafness. Test results relate individually to a particular child's deafness and if you have an understanding of the basic information about hearing tests and measurements of hearing loss, you will be able to relate more easily to the information you are getting from hospitals and audiologists about your child.

Finally, there will be some explanations of the principles relating to various types of hearing aids and other amplification systems. This will be again very basic information as these technical aspects of audiology are a rapidly changing scene and so information about hearing aids etc. are best discussed at the hospital or audiological clinic. Audiology is a complex subject and there is no way to simplify it for people who are new to it while retaining enough accurate information for professionals or those who already have some knowledge. It is impossible to present sufficient and accurate information to satisfy everyone. This is no substitute for using experts in the area who have time to answer specific questions about individual children.

How the ear works

A simple description of the ear and how it functions should help you to understand what can happen to affect that mechanism. The ear is made up of three sections: the outer ear, the middle ear and the inner ear.

The function of the **outer ear** is to collect and trap sound and direct it down the ear canal to the ear drum (tympanic membrane). The ear canal produces wax which protects the ear drum by moving dirt and germs towards the outside of the ear. The ear drum vibrates in response to the external changing sound pressures. It is open to the air but does not allow air or water to pass through.

The ear drum is at the entrance to the **middle ear.** The middle ear is filled with air to keep the air pressure equalised on both sides of the ear drum. The eustachian tube, which opens into the back of the mouth, allows air into the middle ear. Air passes in and out of the middle ear by means of this tube. In the middle ear there are three tiny bones called the ossicles. The vibration of the ear drum causes small movements in these three bones which are interlinked. The linked movement of the bones transmits vibrations from the ear drum to the oval window, which is another membrane similar to the ear drum. This is the entrance to the inner ear.

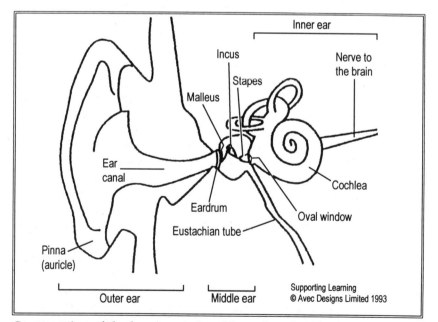

Cross section of the hearing system (Reproduced with permission from Avec Designs Limited)

At the entrance to the **inner ear** the sound vibrations pass from the air in the middle ear into the liquid medium of the inner ear. This fluid converts the sound vibrations from the middle ear into electrical neural impulses. These impulses are then transferred to the auditory centre of the brain via the eighth cranial nerve. The inner ear is in fact a small coiled structure (the cochlear) which is lined by a membrane with hair cells along it and is full of fluid. The inner ear also contains the organs of balance.

Specific parts of the cochlear are sensitive to different pitches of sound. It is here that sounds are first broken down into their individual frequency pattern.

Types of Hearing Loss

Any kind of damage or blockage within the outer or middle ear which causes a reduction in the conduction of sounds through to the inner ear is called a **conductive hearing loss.**

Sounds are perceived as much quieter than they really are. Sometimes the problem is temporary and treatable (such as wax, middle ear infections, or a foreign body) More permanent conductive hearing losses can also be treated and reduced in their effect by the use of hearing aids designed to amplify the sounds arriving at the ear drum.

A major cause of conductive deafness in young children is **glue ear (otitis media).** Glue ear is very common condition in children, especially under the age of five. It is something which most children grow out of. From a linguistic and educational point of view, the early years are essential for language development and learning. Consequently, conductive deafness as a result of glue ears may have an adverse effect on language development and education if allowed to go undetected and untreated in the early years. For a fuller explanation of glue ear see the Appendix (Andrews and Roberts 1994).

Damage to the inner ear results in permanent deafness and is known as **sensori-neural or nerve deafness.** This type of deafness produces distortions in sound perceptions as well as the reduction in sound that we normally think of as deafness. This type of deafness is as a result of damage to the cochlear or to the nerve of deafness. This damage is nearly always permanent and currently there is no remedial treatment.

Recently, however, **cochlear implantation** has become more widespread as a way of restoring some hearing to very deaf children. This procedure does not repair damaged hearing or in any way 'restore' normal hearing but it can offer some experience of sound to profoundly deaf children. There will be further discussion of cochlear implants later in this chapter.

It is possible to have both sensori-neural deafness and conductive deafness at the same time. This condition is known as a **mixed hearing loss**.

Causes of Deafness

The causes of deafness can largely be divided into two categories. Those that the child is born with or **congenital hearing losses** and those that are **an acquired hearing loss** after they are born.

Congenital conductive hearing losses are caused by, e.g;

- a congenital abnormality in the structure of the ear, e.g. Downs syndrome;
- a poorly formed or absent external ear.

Acquired conductive hearing losses are caused by, e.g.,

- wax,
- middle ear infection,
- perforated ear drum,
- trauma.

Congenital sensori-neural hearing losses can be pre-natal or peri-natal and are caused by, e.g.,

(a) Pre-natal (before birth)

- Rhesus incompatibility,
- familial/hereditary factors,
- German measles (rubella),
- severe illness in expectant mothers.

(b) Peri-natal (around birth)

- prematurity
- anoxia
- jaundice

Acquired sensori-neural hearing losses are caused by, e.g.,

- meningitis,
- measles,
- head injury,
- ototoxins.

In summary, in conductive deafness all sounds are perceived as more quiet. It is usually treatable and also responds very well to all amplification devices.

Sensori-neural deafness is usually permanent and sounds are perceived as both distorted and quieter. Hearing aids need to be carefully programmed to amplify sounds appropriately for children with sensori-neural hearing losses.

Testing the Degree of Deafness

It is not enough simply to know that your child has a hearing loss. It is important to know to what degree the pitch (frequency) and loudness (intensity) of the sounds they hear are affected. For this reason their hearing is tested to diagnose the degree and type of deafness to ensure appropriate aids to hearing are prescribed

The terminology you will meet that is used to describe loudness (intensity) of sound and pitch (frequency) is as follows.

Loudness (intensity)

It is important to know how loud a sound has to be before it can be heard. The loudness of any particular sound is measured in decibels (dB). This is the common unit of measurement for the loudness of sounds. The quietest sound the normally hearing ear can detect is established at 0 dB The loudest sound the normally hearing ear can tolerate (pain threshold) is in the order of 140 dB.

The decibel scale is not a familiar one, so the following example gives a rough indication of how it relates to 'real life' with particular reference to the sounds of speech.

Sound intensity in decibels (dB)

0 dB	the quietest sound the healthy ear can detect (pin drop)
20 dB	a whisper at 1 metre
40 dB	a quiet conversation
60 dB	normal conversation
80 dB	a shout
100 dB	a road drill
120 dB	an aircraft taking off
140 dB	normal threshold of pain

Loudness is not the only factor affecting whether we can hear speech. The particular frequency or pitch of the sound makes a big difference to what is heard.

Frequency (pitch)

Frequency (pitch) is measured in Hertz (Hz). The term 'Hertz' is used to describe the number of cycles (sound waves) per second in any tone. For example a tone of 250 Hz would complete 250 cycles per second while the tones of a higher frequency would complete more cycles per second e.g. 4000 Hz would complete 4000 cycles per second. As a rough guide, middle C on the piano is about 256 Hz. The healthy human ear is capable of hearing sounds from 20 Hz (very low sounds) to 20,000 Hz (very high sounds) but the frequencies of speech fall usually between 125 and 8000 Hz. and the most important speech frequencies fall between **250 and 4000 Hz.**

Speech frequencies vary across the speech range from the low-frequency vowel sounds (u or o) and nasal sounds (n or m) to the higher frequency consonant sounds (f, s, sh).

Low-frequency sounds (25–500 Hz)		Middle-frequency sounds (500–2000 Hz)		High-frequency sounds (2000–8000 Hz)	
a	as in cat	ay	as in day	s	as in sink
oo	as in mood	ee	as in weed	sh	as in ship
ow	as in bow	d	as in do	f	as in fence
or	as in bored	m	as in mouse	th	as in think

In general terms the vowels (lower-frequency sounds of speech) contribute power to speech and information about rhythm and intonation. The consonants (higher-frequency sounds) contribute to the intelligibility of speech and give the meaning.

For example, look at the following two sentences

(1) I a- -oi-- -o -e- -o-e --ee--.

This is a simple sentence with all the high-frequency consonant sounds removed. It takes a lot of understanding (unless you are particularly good at decoding).

Here is the same sentence with the low-frequency vowels removed and the consonants added. It should be much easier to understand.

(2) - -m g--ng t- g-t s-m- sw--ts.

Although this is a written sentence we know that hearing functions in a similar way and that it is very hard to understand the spoken word when the consonant sounds are not heard.

Audiograms

When a child's hearing is tested the results are plotted on an audiogram. When a hearing test is carried out, the sound level at which a range of frequencies are heard is plotted on an audiogram. The audiogram form looks like this.

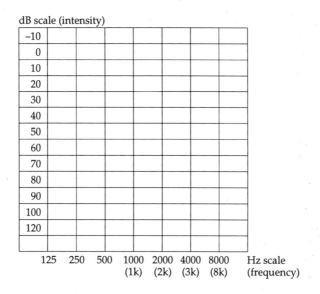

Description

The vertical axis on the audiogram records the loudness of sound. The quietest sound the normally hearing people can hear will be in the region of 0–10 dB. Normal hearing is generally defined as 20 dB or better.

The horizontal axis records the frequency of sounds important to the understanding of speech (usually between 250–4000 kHz). Normally hearing people will detect sounds across all the frequency range.

The hearing levels of both ears are usually plotted on the same audiogram form. The commonly accepted procedure is that the right ear is represented by **O** and the left ear represented by **X**. The left and right points are joined separately to give a graphic representation of the hearing losses indicated in the following tables.

The outlined part of Audiogram A shows the area known as the speech curve. The sounds of normal speech characteristically fall into this area. When the hearing thresholds fall below this area some or all components of speech will be reduced in intensity or lost altogether.

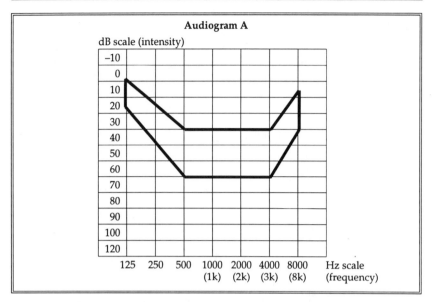

Degree of Hearing Loss

The following audiograms are examples of different degrees and types of hearing loss.

Example 1 This audiogram shows that the child has hearing within normal limits. Any variation between 0–20 dB is considered to be **normal hearing**.

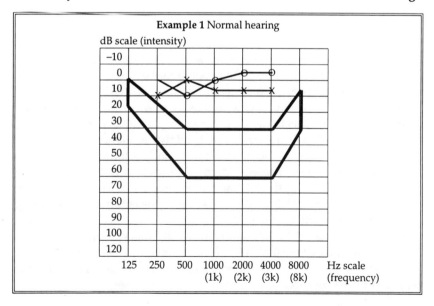

Example 2 This audiogram shows a **mild hearing loss** in both ears and the average loss in the better ear falls between 20 and 40 dB. This type of loss is often called a 'flat loss' in that it is more or less horizontal to the frequency axis and is characteristic of a conductive hearing loss.

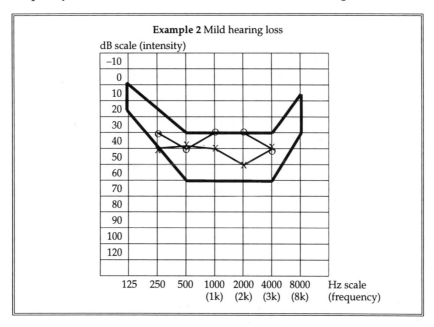

Example 3 This hearing loss is a **moderate hearing loss** and the average loss in the better ear falls between 41 and 70 dB. This type of hearing loss may be flat or can vary across the frequency range. It may be either a conductive or a sensori-neural loss. This type of loss falls largely within the speech area but it means that normal speech is just entering their threshold of hearing so will be only faintly heard.

Example 4 This loss is a **severe hearing loss** with the average loss in the better ear falling between 71 and 95 dB. The hearing in this type of loss falls outside the speech area,. A child with this type of loss would hear very little of any general conversation around them. They would be aware of the louder sounds around them such as lorries and noisy machine.

Example 5 This is a **profound hearing loss** with the average loss in the better ear falling below 95 dB. This shows a profound hearing loss in the middle and low frequencies and no measurable hearing in the high frequencies. Children with this type of loss will not hear anything of speech and even

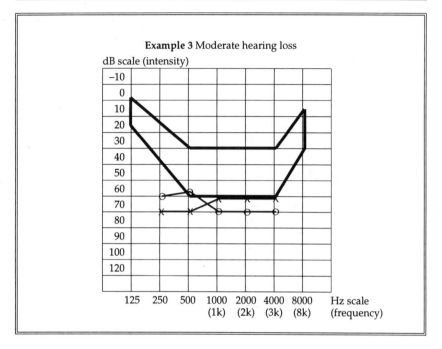

Example 3 Moderate hearing loss

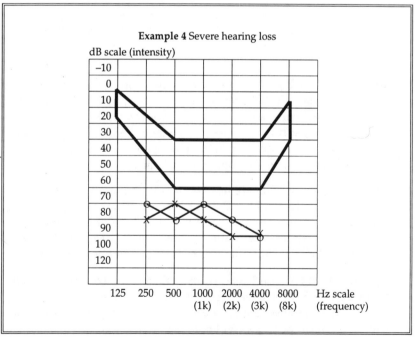

Example 4 Severe hearing loss

with hearing aids they will hear a distorted pattern of speech. These children will rely very heavily on their visual skills to help them communicate.

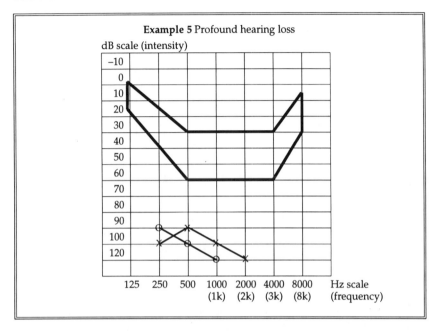

Example 5 Profound hearing loss

Example 6 This audiogram shows a **typical sensori-neural hearing loss** which is hard to categorise although it is very common. The hearing in the low frequencies is more or less normal but that in the high frequencies falls into the profound category. The effect of this type of loss is that the child will hear the low frequency sounds of speech. These are the vowel sounds which give volume and rhythm to speech. However they will hear little of the high frequency, consonant sounds which give intelligibility to speech. Commonly children with this type of loss will begin to talk at the usual time but their expressive speech will sound 'different' as some speech sounds will be missing. It is hard to find appropriate hearing aids for this type of loss although the further development of 'transpositional hearing aids' will go some way to alleviating the problem.

These are a few examples of typical audiograms and the terminology you will meet when you are confronted with your child's particular audiogram. It must be remembered that every audiogram is individual to the particular child and these audiograms are just a guide to the general terms.

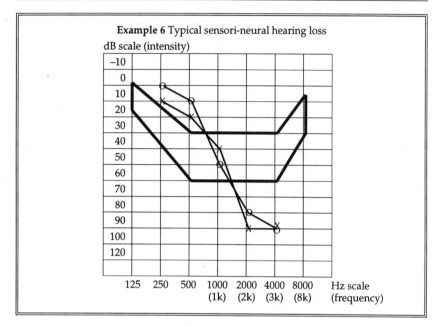

Example 6 Typical sensori-neural hearing loss
dB scale (intensity)

Testing for Hearing Loss

Testing for hearing loss can now be carried out on very young children. This type of test is called neo-natal screening. It is often carried out on young babies who are thought, at birth, to be at risk of having a hearing loss. There is some debate about the value of this becoming a routine test.

More usually deafness is discovered in babies via a routine screening test administered by for example, health visitors. Often however, parents have been concerned about their child and have sought help for themselves. Sometimes parents feel guilty because they had not suspected any problem with their child. There is absolutely no reason to blame yourself if you had not registered a difference. Many deaf children become very visually aware and communicate and interact in a very comprehensive way.

All testing of deaf children, at any age, is designed to establish their threshold of hearing but clearly young children are not able to perform complicated test routines.

The testing of children under the age of about 6 months is called **behavioural observation audiometry** (BOA) and relies upon an observation of the child's behaviour in response to exposure to sounds the level of which is carefully monitored.

The early tests on young children, that is from when a child can sit up and has head control until they are about 18 months, are called **distraction**

tests. This test requires two people; one to hold the attention of the child with toys or other objects to the front and the other to present a sound stimulus out of the visual field of the baby. This test depends upon the distractibility of the young by toys and their reflex action in response to sound stimulus. The sounds presented give an approximation of low- and high-frequency sounds at different frequencies. Often a high-frequency rattle is used and the low sounds are presented as an OO sound.

After about 18 months children's awareness of sound is well developed and so they are no longer reliably distracted by sounds. At this stage it is anticipated that children should be able to follow simple instructions using toys as stimulus; for example, 'Give it to Mummy' or 'Put it in the box'. These tests are called **cooperative tests**.

Depending upon the stage of development, children from about 3 years can be expected to perform a simple task in response to the word GO (a low-frequency sound) and SS (a high-frequency sound). These tests are called **performance tests.** The child is taught to wait for a sound and then respond in a play activity such as putting a man in the train or a brick in a box.

Once a child is used to performing reliably and regularly , then it is possible to undertake **free field or pure tone audiometry** within a hospital setting where much more accurate audiometric testing is possible. This involves the same principles as performance testing except that the sound is presented through headphones worn by the child. Clearly this allows for much more accurate levels of hearing loss to be defined.

Summary of test procedures

The ages given for the various test procedures are approximate and depend upon the child's stage of development.

Under 6 months — *Behavioural observation audiometry (BOA)*
6–18 months — *Distraction tests*
18 months – 3 years — *Cooperative tests.*
3 years onwards — *Performance tests.*
3½ years onwards — *Free field or pure tone audiometry*

All the tests described here require the child being tested to make a response, either an automatic reflex response as in the distraction test or a conditioned response of some type. They also depend upon the tester to make a subjective judgement about that response.

Objective tests which do not require the child to make a response but merely to cooperate with the test procedures are also used. The responses are monitored and recorded by the equipment used. The two most common tests are Electric Response Audiometry and the tympanogram.

In **electric response audiometry** the brain's response to sound signals presented by the placement of electrodes behind each ear is measured. It is totally painless and does not require the child to respond in any way except to remain relatively still. For this reason this test is sometimes administered under an anaesthetic with very young children.

For children who have problems in the middle ear such as glue ear or catarrh, then a **tympanogram** may be taken. Again this does not require the child to do anything except sit relatively still. A small probe is put in the ear which tests the equality of the air pressure between the outer and middle ear. This test can confirm whether the deafness is a conductive deafness or not.

Although you may feel that your child has had to undergo a great many testing procedures it is important to understand that the level of deafness cannot always be confirmed by one test alone. The diagnosis of deafness does not depend on a single test. With young children a combination of subjective and objective tests should be carried out. Also observational evidence from both parents and other involved professionals all contribute to assessing accurately the level of deafness and how each individual child responds to their deafness and to their hearing aids.

Hearing Aids

Hearing aids come in a variety of shapes, sizes and types. Common types of hearing aids for children are body-worn aids, post-aural aids, in-the-ear aids, aids mounted on spectacles. The type that most parents are likely to come into contact with are body-worn and post-aural hearing aids. Hearing aids are all relatively simple devices and have the same essential component parts.

They consist of:

- a microphone which collects sounds and converts them into electrical impulses,
- an amplifier which increases the sound energy via a volume control,
- a receiver which changes the electrical impulses back into sound waves (amplified),
- a lead (in a body worn aid or an elbow and tubing (in post aural aid),
- an ear mould (individually made) which connects the receiver to the hearing aid wearer,
- a battery to power this system.

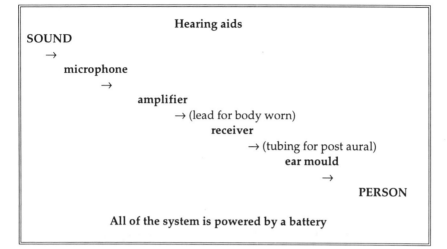

Hearing aids

SOUND
→
microphone
→
amplifier
→ (lead for body worn)
receiver
→ (tubing for post aural)
ear mould
→
PERSON

All of the system is powered by a battery

Hearing-aid technology is advancing all the time but it is still true that a hearing aid is only that — an aid to hearing. It does *not* restore hearing to the level the normally hearing person can hear. It has certain limitations.

Firstly, most hearing aids are not specifically tuned to speech sounds in the way that the human ear is. This means that all sounds are amplified and the background noise can be loud and disturbing and apparently mask speech sounds (newly developing digital hearing aids are attempting to address this problem).

Secondly, children with more severe and profound hearing losses may find the trouble and discomfort that hearing aids can cause outweighs the auditory information they obtain through wearing them.

What is clear is that all deaf children should be encouraged to wear their hearing aids. This is to ensure that they are given the maximum opportunity to fully utilise their own residual hearing. Obviously in the early days this will require a lot of support, encouragement and management from parents. Nobody has ever said that this is an easy job. What is true is that given support and encouragement in the beginning then most deaf children and adults wear their hearing aids happily if they are beneficial to them.

Wearing hearing aids is not always a straightforward issue. We have to consider, for instance, the teenager for whom hearing aids may be an embarrassment or young people who are very linked to their deaf identity and feel that wearing hearing aids may negate that position.

For children with some useful residual hearing, the use of hearing aids can be very important providing a degree of access to the spoken language of parents and siblings.

Introduction and management of hearing aids should be achieved by parents in conjunction with and support from the relevant professionals at the hospital and by the visiting teacher in the home.

Recent advances in hearing aid technology are in the areas of digital hearing aids which aim to be selective in amplification and dual microphone hearing aids which help to combat the difficulties of background noise.

Transpositional hearing aids aim to address problem of amplification for hearing losses which have no response to high frequency sounds.

Radio aids

A radio hearing aid effectively 'reduces' the distance between the speaker and the deaf child, whether that speaker is a parent, teacher or anyone in communication with the child. In the usual post-aural hearing aid the microphone is close to the ear of the person wearing the aid. As we have said, this microphone picks up and amplifies all background noise as well as speech. It cannot discriminate between the two. The microphone on a post aural hearing aid becomes less and less effective as the distance between the speaker and the child increases.

In a radio aid the microphone is separated from the hearing aid and given to the speaker. The subsequent link between the microphone and the receiver on the child's ear is via radio waves.

This means that the distance between the spoken word and the microphone is close and constant and there is less opportunity for background noise to be picked and therefore interfere with the speech sounds. The signal transmitted to the hearing aid remains at a constant level regardless of the distance between the speaker and the child.

For these reasons radio aids are particularly beneficial to deaf children in classrooms where there is a lot of background noise. They are also useful outside where the distance between speaker and the child may be greater.

They do have many advantages over post-aural hearing aids, as described earlier, but still they remain an aid to hearing and do not return the hearing to normal.

Cochlear Implants

A cochlear implant is a surgical procedure where a set of electrodes are implanted directly into the cochlear in the inner ear. This implant then effectively by-passes the inner ear and electrically stimulates directly the nerve of hearing.

As with any other hearing aid there are also external parts to the system. They consists of a microphone which collects sounds from the environment and converts then into an electrical impulses, this is similar to any post-aural hearing aid.

In addition to the conventional hearing aid the system includes a speech processor, which is body worn, usually in a belt at the waist. This converts the electrical signal from the microphone in a form which can be delivered to the electrode in the implant.

The signal from the speech processor is delivered through a lead to the electrode in the implant via a plug fixed surgically into the skull.

A cochlear implant benefits some deaf children by giving them the sensation of 'hearing'. For this hearing to become meaningful and pleasurable requires a large commitment on the part of the family and others working with the child. The rehabilitation programme, which is directed, primarily towards developing listening skills is considered to be as important as the operation itself and without that the implant system is not fully effective.

There are several issues related to cochlear implantation which need to be aired. Realistically, cochlear implants are very expensive, any surgery is potentially dangerous and cochlear implantation takes place very near to the facial nerves. They are particularly suitable for those deafened children and adults who already have a memory for the spoken word. For them, the stimulus transmitted by the implant relates well to their previous knowledge of language and can be a useful aid.

It is more problematical when considering the implantation of deaf children or adults who have never had access to sound and therefore have no previous knowledge of the sound system of the particular spoken language of their society. The auditory information given via the implant may be insufficient to fully perceive the spoken language and therefore the task of learning the spoken language may be enormous. The results of implantation in these situations have yet to be realised.

In this current climate of acknowledgement of human rights, many deaf people and others involved in the education of deaf children argue that a decision by parents to implant their deaf children violates the rights of the child by performing 'unnecessary' surgery on them. They argue that the risks of irreversible implant surgery are too great and any natural residual hearing is completely destroyed.

Cochlear Implants and Sign Language

Currently the status of cochlear implantation for children who are already developing sign language is a developing one. There is an assumption that once a child has had an implant then all the subsequent support for language development and education should reflect the oral/aural approach.

The majority of children suitable for implantation are likely to be in the profoundly deaf category and may already be developing sign language as a first language. In some geographical areas this may not be an option. If the option to develop sign language is there, then the issue of cochlear implants for potential sign language using children is a very important one.

The issue for sign language using deaf children, or sign bilingual deaf children, is that the development of spoken and written English as a first or second language is of a high priority. If the insertion of a cochlear implant will enhance those skills, then it certainly has a place within bilingual education.

The issue is that the rehabilitation programme devised for children with cochlear implants should rightly concentrate on developing the spoken language of deaf children. However, it should not be instead of their developing sign language but should complement it. Currently new areas of research seem to suggest that deaf children, with cochlear implants who use sign language, do as well, and sometimes better, in developing their English skills as those deaf children who have only been exposed to spoken language. This would reflect many of the known factors about bilingualism; that is, the development of a second language is enhanced by the firm acquisition of a first language.

A cochlear implant is yet another form of hearing aid and, as such, cannot restore hearing to normal levels. It has a place, as with other amplification devices, in enhancing the linguistic opportunity and educational development of bilingual deaf children. It may give added opportunity to develop listening skills and spoken language in deaf children as either their first or second language.

Conclusion

Audiology has an undisputed place in the development and education of all deaf children. Accurate diagnosis of hearing loss and appropriate amplification is the right of all deaf children. This is no less true for developing bilingual deaf children as the aim of bilingualism is the development of two languages to their fullest potential. In the case of deaf children these languages are a signed language and the spoken language of their community. There can only be opportunity for the development of these two languages if children have fullest access to both through interaction with sign language using adults and fullest and most up-to-date audiological support.

Additional Reading

McCracken, W. and Sutherland, H. (1991) *Deaf Ability not Disability.* Clevedon: Multilingual Matters
  Chapter 3 'Aids to Hearing'. This chapter gives a very good overview of the types of hearing aid and guidance to parents on the management of hearing aids in young children

McCormick, B., Archbold, S. and Sheppard, S. (1995) *Cochlear Implants for Young Children.* London: Whurr.
  This edited book, written by members of the Cochlear Implant Team in Nottingham explains and describes implantation in detail.

LASER (1995) *Cochlear Implantation and Bilingualism.* London: LASER Publications.
  This report is a series of papers given by deaf people, a teenager with an implant and his family, members of a cochlear implant team and relevant statistics   related to cochlear implants.

Chapter 2

Ways of Looking at Deafness

In this chapter, the intention is for us to move on from the purely medical or audiological aspects of deafness and consider another way of looking at it. Through the exploration of two different **models of deafness** we can consider aspects of deafness from a medical point of view or as a **medical model** or from a language point of view, that is a **linguistic model**. We can then reflect on what deafness means medically and also what it means for the language, the social and the educational development of deaf children.

Medical Model of Deafness?

When it is suspected that any child, for whatever reason, may have some degree of deafness the next step for the family usually involves a visit to the hospital Ear, Nose and Throat (ENT) Department. A series of tests, probably over several visits, will take place. From these tests it is possible to diagnose or establish the child's degree of deafness. This diagnosis of hearing loss will classify the degree of deafness into one of several categories called **audiological descriptors**. This means the child will be diagnosed as being mildly, moderately, severely or profoundly deaf. Generally those children whose deafness falls within the categories of mild, moderate and less severe will be thought of as a 'partially deaf' child while those whose deafness is in the more severe and profound category will be considered to be a 'profoundly deaf' child. Efforts will also be made to find the cause of the problem and to provide appropriate amplification devices (hearing aids) to compensate for the degree of deafness as far as is possible. This way of describing and defining deafness reflects a medical perspective. Implicit in this view of deafness is that it is regarded first and foremost as a medical condition of greater or lesser severity depending on the diagnosis and therefore emphasis is placed on appropriate medical treatment and the provision of hearing aids. Both of these actions are to cure or minimise the effects of deafness.

Linguistic Model of Deafness?

An alternative model of deafness is one which, while accepting and addressing the medical implications of deafness, primarily focuses on the 'linguistic needs' of the deaf child. Here consideration is given to the language (spoken or signed) the deaf child will most easily and fully develop to a level related to their age and general development. It is appreciated that there are many external factors influencing the linguistic development of a deaf child, including the hearing status of the family, social, environmental and economic factors. However the focus remains on their specific language needs and the language they would acquire most easily and appropriately for their age. This can be thought of in terms of the child's **first or preferred language**. It is generally accepted that the most common indicator of a deaf child's developing preferred language will be their degree of deafness. It is accepted that those children who are partially deaf will probably have enough residual hearing to develop a spoken language as their preferred means of communication. A child who is diagnosed as profoundly deaf is more likely to develop sign language — the visual/gestural language of the deaf community — as their preferred mode of communication. So the condition of deafness can be thought of as a 'linguistic model' where some deaf children use spoken English as their first language and develop sign language as a second language and others who use sign language as a first language and English (or the spoken language of the country where they are born) as their second language. This can replace a medical model where children are categorised by their degree of deafness.

In the context of this book the focus is not solely upon deafness as a medical condition, but more particularly upon the language needs of the child arising from their specific pattern of deafness and their language preferences.

The next part of this chapter will look at the implications of both of these models in more detail but, first of all, let us consider some of the initial reactions to deafness in the family.

Family Reactions to Deafness

The emotional impact experienced by all families, when they discover that they have a child who is deaf, cannot be underestimated. Reactions are typically strong but variable. For most deaf families, there will be joy and pleasure in a baby who will grow up sharing their language and culture. 'Bringing up baby' will be viewed with pleasure with no anticipation of anything other than the accepted ups and downs of family life. Where one parent is deaf and the other hearing a similar reaction may follow although one couple in this situation admitted to 'a slight disappointment and adjustment' on discovering that their child is deaf. For one partially hearing mother with a profoundly deaf husband, the fact that their third child was diagnosed profoundly deaf after having one partially hearing and one hearing child produced very mixed feelings. While the father was totally accepting of the profoundly deaf baby, the mother was concerned at this 'third dimension' — a profoundly deaf child — in the family.

Each family will have individual responses and needs to having a deaf child, but it is generally accepted that the reactions of deaf and hearing parents will be different and most deaf parents will respond more positively to the birth of a deaf child than hearing parents.

For a hearing family the initial reactions to the discovery that their child is deaf are typically, and understandably, negative, emotional and very strong. The vast majority (90%) of deaf children are born to hearing families. Many such families may never have met a deaf person or child. The needs of hearing parents at that time are to have the opportunity to assimilate the situation and to work through the negative feelings which may well include grief and anger. They need people to talk to who have had experiences similar to their own and they need appropriate and timely information. There will be many questions arising around the whole issue of deafness and the implications for the family and for their child.

Questions Related to Medical Aspects of Deafness

The following are some of the most commonly asked questions by parents at this time which are closely related to a medical model of deafness.

Why is my child deaf?

Once parents realise that their child is deaf, it is very natural for them to want to know why. What has caused deafness in their child? While there are many known causes of deafness, it is important to say at this stage that, in up to approximately 60% of all cases, the specific cause of deafness is never discovered. So for many the quest may well be fruitless. Where the cause is known, there are two broad categories to be considered. One is when deafness is present at birth (congenital deafness) and the second is when deafness is acquired after the birth (acquired deafness). Congenital deafness may be as a result of family history, genetic issues, viruses during pregnancy, difficulties of prematurity or other problems surrounding the birth. Acquired deafness occurs from childhood illnesses such as meningitis, measles and mumps, by side effects from certain drugs, from head injuries or from continuing infections of the middle ear.

Will it get better? Can it be cured?

This is a very natural question to ask and again any explanation falls roughly into two categories related to the two categories of deafness. Firstly there is what is called conductive deafness caused largely by infections of the middle ear and this usually responds positively to medical or surgical treatment. Secondly there is sensori-neural deafness caused by damage to the inner ear, the cochlear or the nerve pathways to the brain. Damage in these areas currently has to be considered as permanent. This means it is not going to improve and, on the whole, it is unlikely to deteriorate.

What is the difference between conductive deafness and sensori-neural deafness?

Deafness caused by factors affecting the outer or middle ear is called conductive deafness because effectively sound waves are prevented, for a variety of reasons, from being conducted through the outer and middle ear to the inner ear. On the whole, only the loudness or the quantity of sound arriving at the inner ear is reduced. Sensori-neural deafness or nerve deafness is caused by damage to the inner ear where sound waves are converted into electrical impulses or damage to the acoustic nerve, which transmits sound to the brain. Any damage in these areas results in not only a reduction in the quantity of sound received, but also the quality of sound received is affected. However loud the sound is, if a child has a sensori-neural deafness they will hear a reduced and distorted pattern of that sound.

Will my child be able to hear when they get a hearing aid?

Hearing aids are exactly that. They are an aid to hearing. What they can do is to amplify or make sounds louder. They are small, powerful and very sophisticated and can be adjusted to suit different types of deafness So for conductive deafness, where the mechanism of hearing is intact but the sound is not being conducted to the inner ear, they are particularly effective. In sensori-neural deafness, when the mechanism is either damaged or not functioning properly, they are still helpful but not as effective. In any situation a hearing aid cannot reproduce 'normal' hearing, but it can increase a child's experience of sound.

Will my child learn to talk?

There is no easy, straightforward answer to this question. All deaf children (except in a very few cases) do have some hearing, however slight. It is through the use of this residual hearing plus the use of hearing aids that deaf children are able to develop their spoken language. However, the level to which children can develop spoken language is variable and depends on many factors including, for example, their experience of language and their own urge to communicate. However, it is generally accepted that their degree of deafness is the most influential factor plus the use the individual child is able to make of whatever hearing s/he has. It is likely that those children falling within the mild/moderate and severe categories of deafness will develop spoken language alongside their hearing peers and that it will become their preferred mode of communication. Profoundly deaf children may develop some spoken language but it will take longer and is unlikely to be the language with which they feel most comfortable or can fully express their thoughts and feelings. It is important to understand that the development of spoken language for all deaf children is likely to be relatively slower than that of their hearing peers.

Will I be able to 'talk' to him/her if she can't hear me?

Yes you can, but you need to appreciate that so much of 'talking' to young children is not necessarily in words. So it is better not to think in terms of talking and hearing. The term 'easy communication' offers a much broader view of all the interactions between parents and children. This includes talking but also acknowledges the place of physical contact, facial expression, gestures and all the other facets of any parent interacting with their child. It is important to remember that deaf children rely heavily upon visual information and so in any communicative situation it is essential that they have the maximum opportunity to 'see' what is happening, to have the fullest possible information from any 'talking' that happens.

Where will s/he go to school?

All children are individual and when they are very young it is not possible to predict, accurately, how they will develop or what type of educational support they will need. Deaf children are no exception to this so it is inappropriate to decide at a young age where they should attend school. It is important to see how the child develops and then to consider how their educational needs may best be met. There is a range of educational options from going to their local mainstream school with some support from specialist teachers, attending a mainstream school which is not local but will have other deaf children, special units attached to mainstream schools and there are special schools for deaf children. These schools are either within the local education authority or run independently. Every option needs to be considered in relation to the developing linguistic and educational needs of the child .

What is a cochlear implant?

Briefly a cochlear implant can be thought of as another aid to hearing. Part of the aid is implanted into the mastoid bone and part is worn on the body. It works as a hearing aid by directly stimulating the nerve of hearing through electrical signals in response to environmental and speech sounds. It cannot restore hearing and the sounds reaching the brain are limited and distorted. It cannot work efficiently if there is damage to either the auditory nerve or to the central processing area of the brain. (For more information about cochlear implants see Chapter 1.)

Will my daughter/son get married?

Most adult deaf people do get married in roughly the same proportion as hearing people. Deaf people often marry other deaf people although it is not unusual for deaf and hearing people to marry.

Will they be able to drive a car when they grow up?

Yes. There is absolutely no reason, because of their deafness, for a deaf person not to drive a car!

Will s/he be able to get a job?

Recently published figures about young deaf people stated that 75% of young deaf people were in or had been in some form of employment, job scheme or sheltered employment. This figure is very comparable with general employment figures for young people. Young deaf people can expect the same employment opportunities as hearing young people. Also all deaf young people are entitled to the same further education opportunities as their hearing brothers and sisters.

These and many other questions (considered later in the book) inevitably flow through the minds of hearing parents in the early days of discovering that they have a deaf child. Certainly much of the information, particularly audiological information, is available in this book. However given the need for information combined with a need to talk to other people in a similar situation then meeting with other parents and families who have common shared experiences is a most helpful way to proceed.

Questions relating to the broader issues of life-style and expectations for their children are often best answered by deaf people themselves and those who work constantly with deaf people. It is important for parents to meet deaf children and deaf adults as quickly as possible so that many of their questions and concerns about their own child can be explored with people with first-hand knowledge and experience of the very issues that are concerning them. It can be a positive and affirming experience for both parents and children to meet deaf adults who will probably be married and most likely to be driving a car!

The deaf adults that families meet may well be using sign language as their means of communication and this may at first feel both unnerving and confusing. Sign language is the visual gestural language of the deaf community; a complete language with its' own grammar and structure. It is expressed through a combination of signs, finger spelling, facial expression and body movement. It is a separate language from the spoken language of the community, although this language does in some ways influence the sign language of the particular country. However, many deaf adults are very used to communicating with hearing people and have well developed ways of making themselves understood.

Introducing the Issues of a Linguistic Model of Deafness

The fundamental principle to be considered when viewing deafness as a linguistic issue is that all children, deaf and hearing, have the right to the fullest opportunity to develop a language at an age-appropriate level in relation to their general development. For hearing children this will be a spoken language, the first language of the home environment. For deaf children from deaf families who use sign language, it will be sign language, the first language of their home.

For deaf children from hearing families the picture is not so clear. Developing a spoken language may well be the case depending upon the child's degree of deafness. Some deaf children may well develop the spoken language of the home. But what is important is that all deaf children, whether from deaf or hearing families, are given the opportunity to experience the range of language options available to deaf people from spoken to the sign language of the deaf community. In the UK this is British Sign Language (BSL). With this opportunity they will be able to establish and develop their own linguistic preferences. For profoundly deaf children from hearing families it is particularly important that they should have experience of sign language or a language with sign support so that they may have experience of a language to which they can respond at an appropriate time.

It is likely that those deaf children who have a mild/moderate or severe hearing loss will develop spoken language as their preferred or first language but may also develop some skill in sign language, if they are given the opportunity, as a second language for use when meeting other deaf children and grown-ups. Some children initially respond to both languages before identifying their first language but still retain some skills in the second language. Other children develop early receptive and expressive skills predominantly in sign language. For them it will become their preferred language but they will also need to develop English, in a spoken and/or written form to function well in the hearing society.

Questions Related to Linguistic Aspects of Deafness

How can I 'expose' my young deaf child 'to a variety of languages?

For both hearing parents and deaf children it is a good idea to meet deaf adults and other deaf children as soon as possible. Not only can they talk about their own life experiences and what it means to be deaf with the family but they can also introduce sign language, if it is appropriate, to the deaf child and the whole family including grandparents if they are around. Regular meetings ensure continual exposure to sign language for the deaf child as well as ongoing experience of spoken English which is the language of the family and home. Many parents begin to develop skills in using sign combined with spoken language quite early on. This is often thought of as a bridge between sign language and spoken language. Young deaf children quickly develop receptive skills for the visual and pre-lingual aspects of sign language such as facial expression, pointing and the development of increasingly sustained eye contact. (In the same way hearing children understand and respond to the spoken word before they learn to produce recognisable sounds and words.) In this way deaf children can experience both signed and spoken languages. This type of exposure can extend beyond the family into other settings such as playgroups and nurseries where the presence of deaf adults as part of the nursery team ensure that deaf children are exposed to sign language as well as spoken language in educational as well as home settings.

How do the children know which is their preferred language?

Language development in young children is a wide and complex subject but it is generally accepted that as children's language skills develop, their understanding of what is being signed or spoken to them (their receptive skills) develops ahead of their ability to respond through either the spoken word or sign (their expressive skills). It is possible to monitor their developing language skills in both sign and spoken language. For some children, it is very clear which language is developing more quickly and fully and it is likely that more profoundly deaf children will develop the visual gestural language that is sign language more quickly. Other children who are less deaf will usually develop spoken language more quickly. However, many deaf children, who are able to make more use of their residual hearing may well develop both spoken and signed languages at the same time although at different levels of skill. As the child's linguistic skills develop this distinction between the two languages becomes more obvious and the child intuitively relates more fully to the language in which they can most easily communicate their needs and with which they feel most comfortable. Many young deaf children who are developing skills in both languages can switch between the two depending on whether they are with deaf or hearing children or people.

So although we talk about children 'knowing' which language they prefer to use, it is actually a case of children using and developing the language they can most easily learn, use most effectively and with which they are most comfortable. This is not a conscious decision but one which they naturally and intuitively arrive at for themselves.

How will we be able to communicate with our child?

Communication between parents and children is a developing process and it is much more than simple learning of words and signs. It includes all aspects of communication, non- verbal as well as verbal, such as touch, context and facial expression. As a child's preferred mode of communication emerges it is possible for parents to reflect that emerging language. If young children are displaying some skills in sign language alongside their developing English or their first language is emerging as sign language then it is possible for parents and families to learn sign language alongside their deaf child. It is important to remember that communication is a two-way process between parents and children and other members of the family. In reality, most parents who begin to learn sign language use a combination of speech and sign within the family.

This is not necessarily a daunting task as many of the early pre-lingual features of sign language are easy to add into the communicative process without disrupting the normal conversational flow. Many of the features of simplified early communication between hearing parents and their hearing babies, known as 'motherese' or child-directed language are seen in the sign language communications between deaf parents and their deaf babies. The sign language used by deaf people with their young children is simplified, often slower and the content is usually in relation to the babies' needs and interests just as any hearing parents talk to their young children. The response from deaf babies and children, for whom sign language is emerging as their first language, to any form of sign language is positive, overwhelming and motivation enough for parents to continue to develop their own skills.

Case Examples

Here are some case histories which illustrate how children may be exposed to a 'variety of linguistic experiences' within the family and in nursery and how their language has developed from these experiences. The hearing status of the members of the family are in bold and the language used by that person is in italics. If the child and the family has also met with a deaf adult this is also in bold with their language use in italics. This will give a picture of the range of languages experienced by each family.

GILL aged 5 years is profoundly deaf and has a **partially deaf mother** *(spoken English)* and a **profoundly deaf father** *(sign language)*. She has had home visits from a **deaf adult** *(sign language)*. She attends a mainstream school with **deaf and hearing peers and staff** *(sign language and spoken English)*.

Gill has developed sign language as her first/preferred language, she is now beginning to develop some spoken language, her literacy skills are developing well.

JOHN aged 5 years is profoundly deaf and has a **hearing mother** *(spoken English and developing sign language)*. He has regular visits from a deaf adult *(sign language)*. He attends mainstream school with **deaf and hearing peers** *(sign language and spoken English)*.

John has developed sign language as his preferred language with some emerging English through reading and writing

---

PETER aged 4 years is moderately deaf and has **hearing parents** *(spoken English)*. He has had some visits from a **deaf adult** *(sign language)*.
He attends mainstream nursery with **deaf and hearing staff** *(spoken English and sign language)*.

Peter is developing both spoken English and sign language. His preferred language is emerging as English but he uses some sign language with his deaf peers and adults.

DAVID aged 3 years is partially deaf and has a **partially deaf father** *(spoken English)* and a **hearing mother** *(spoken English)*. He has had a few visits from a **deaf adult** *(sign language)*. He attends mainstream nursery with **deaf and hearing peers and staff** *(spoken English and sign language)*.

David is developing English as his first language. He makes little use of sign language although he has some receptive skills.

KAPRA is 3 years old, is profoundly deaf and has a **hearing mother** *(spoken Urdu)* and a **hearing father** *(spoken English and Urdu)*. He has an older **profoundly deaf brother** *(British Sign Language)* and two hearing sisters *(spoken English and Urdu)*. He has had some visits from a **deaf adult** *(sign language)*. He attends a mainstream nursery with **deaf and hearing staff** *(sign language and spoken English)*.

Kapra is in the situation where he is exposed to three languages. Usually spoken Urdu in the home, some spoken English in the home from his sisters and father and also in the nursery. He meets sign language in the home from a deaf adult and also from his mother and sisters who are beginning to learn sign language themselves.

Kapra is slowly developing sign language skills, with a mixture of 'home signs' and the standard BSL he meets in the nursery. At the moment they are his main way of communicating. He vocalises a lot with accompanying lip patterns which at the moment relate more to Urdu, the spoken language of the home than to English.

From these examples it becomes clear that all the children have developed an identifiable linguistic preference but three of the four are also developing skills in the other or second language. It is also the case that the languages developing and used by deaf children may vary depending upon the situation. For example, they may make more use of sign language when they are with someone with sign language skills but use more English skills when mixing with hearing brothers and sisters.

For *Gill* sign language is her preferred language but English is developing through the spoken and written form as her second or additional language.

For *John* sign language is his preferred language and English is developing through the written form as his second language.

For *Peter* spoken English is his preferred language but he also has well developed skills in sign language.

For *David* spoken English is his preferred language and he has developed minimal sign language skills

For *Kapra* it seems that sign language is his preferred language although it is poorly developed as yet and he is also developing early linguistic skills in Urdu, the main language of his home.

This illustrates four possible examples of the development and use of two languages:

(1) Sign language as the preferred language with English skills (written or spoken) less well developed (Gill and John).
(2) Sign language and English both developed to a level where the child can switch between the two (Peter).

(3) English as the preferred language but with some level of skill in sign language (David).

(4) Sign language as a preferred language and Urdu as a developing second language (Kapra).

This developing use of two (or three) languages is the basis upon which deaf children can be considered in terms of their emerging bilingualism.

Finding a Balance

It is accepted that the medical issues surrounding deafness must be addressed and will continue to be fully addressed. However, if deafness is considered from a 'medical' perspective then the child is viewed as having a medical condition which is diagnosable and treatable with the objective of 'curing' or ameliorating the situation as fully as possible. The implications of this standpoint can be interpreted as the state of deafness as undesirable and the main aim is to compensate for deafness by encouraging a deaf child to function as near to a hearing child as possible. The next logical step on this path is that if the aim is to be as near a hearing child as possible then fullest use of their residual hearing and the development of spoken language must also be the primary aim. It can be argued that if this is the only view taken then the deaf child is immediately put into difficulties where their deafness is denied and all emphases and effort are towards goals that are linked to hearing norms.

Viewing deafness from a linguistic perspective is a different and positive way of considering deafness and deaf children. If the opportunity is there for deaf children to develop their own preferred or first language (and this is acknowledged encouraged and respected) then future plans for their education placement and support can be more easily identified respecting their linguistic and educational needs. It allows the opportunity to address and respect the broader linguistic and linked cultural issues as well as the medical implications.

It is appreciated that there has to be a balance between the importance ascribed to the medical and linguistic models but from now on this book will explore the needs of all deaf children in terms of their preferred language or linguistic status which may spoken English, sign language or a mixture of both.

Summary

This chapter has looked at deafness from two perspectives. One focuses on deafness as a medical condition with the associated emphasis on cure or minimising, as far as possible, the effects of deafness. While medicine residual hearing it is important to remember that some types of deafness are not curable and for some children the exclusive aim of developing spoken language as a first language may be difficult to attain.

The second model which considers deafness as primarily a matter of appropriate language development and maximising the opportunity for all deaf children to develop the most appropriate language at a chronologically matched age.

The medical model of deafness has the following features:

- deafness is a medical condition;
- emphasis on early and accurate diagnosis of deafness;
- emphasis on the use of hearing aids and development of the auditory channel; and
- emphasis on the development of spoken language.

Linguistic model of deafness has the following features.

- focus on identifying the linguistic needs of the child (sign or speech);
- provision of appropriate linguistic experiences;
- development of the preferred language of the child; and
- support for the possible development of two languages.

Additional Reading

Campbell, J. and Oliver, M. (1996) *Disability Politics: Understanding Our Past, Changing Our Future.* London: Routledge.
> This book explores the growth of the disability movement including the perspectives of deaf and disabled people themselves. It also discusses whether the deaf community may or may not fit into the disability movement.

Knight, P. (1998) Disability and deafness. In S. Gregory, P. Knight *et al* (eds.) *Issues in Deaf Education.* London: Fulton Press.
> This chapter refers to general models of disability and how they relate to models of deafness.

Part 2

The Young Deaf Child

The goal of parents and children alike . . . is to maintain comfortable and 'normal' interactions within the home. In this the whole family is involved and has to work together with patience and understanding.

Marschark (1997: 16)

Chapter 3

Family and Professionals

This chapter considers the issues for every family when they have a child who is diagnosed as deaf. The intention is to reflect upon the initial reactions to this situation and then to consider the implications for both deaf children and families. All families and their children need some support at this time. It is important to understand the type of support that is helpful, to consider the support that is available and to ensure that the needs of each individual family are being met. This support comes largely from professional people who work in areas related to deaf education. So this chapter also looks at how parents and professionals can most productively work together.

Introduction

Before we address the issues which directly involve the family of a deaf child we need to appreciate that it is an event of major significance for a hearing family to have a deaf child. While the enormity of the impact on a family must be acknowledged and not underestimated, equally it must not be seen as a totally insurmountable problem. Through support and information, families and particularly parents should be able to relax with, worry about and enjoy their deaf child as much as any other child.

From the abundance of literature, both descriptive and in the personal experiences of parents themselves, as well as through informal conversations it is clear that having a deaf child in the family is a life-changing experience and it is important that the experience should be a positive one and constructive for the whole family.

> It has been a life changing experience . . . met lots of people . . . really had to grow up . . . if was something I could not turn my back on. (Parent in conversation)

The nature of the initial experience will vary for individual families but what is clear, and fundamental to appreciating the issues involved, is that the impact of deafness is not solely on the child but on the whole family. It is as much their reactions and responses to their child's deafness as it is the fact of deafness in itself which will have an impact on the child. It must be acknowledged here that very long-standing, undiagnosed deafness would affect any child and can be a frustrating and potentially disaffecting experience. However, this is not to say that parents should feel either guilty or upset that they had not recognised signs of deafness in their child. Many people feel that time spent in relaxed interaction with their child has been time well spent and there appears to be no firm evidence that those with a later discovery of deafness do less well than those diagnosed much earlier.

It accepted that the following family reactions are more likely to apply to hearing families of deaf children, who are of course the vast majority, than to deaf families. However, it is dangerous always to think of these issues in terms of extremes, as Hillary Sutherland, a deaf parent, reflects in her book

> Deep down I knew he was deaf but to be stone deaf was extremely rare. I was completely taken aback . . . to say I was a bit upset was an understatement. (p. 29)

While it is accepted that all parents of deaf children will have individual reactions and needs, in general those reactions of deaf and hearing parents will be different. It is usually accepted that deaf parents will respond more positively to the birth of a deaf child than hearing parents. In most deaf families the fact that the child is deaf is accepted and welcomed as the norm and the whole process of parenting continues in a natural and uninterrupted way. There is a common mode of communication in the household and little disruption to the natural interactive process between parents and the deaf child. So the child's natural course of development and child/parent bonding is not adversely affected.

This uninterrupted parenting pattern, which occurs between deaf parents and their deaf child, is often offered as the reason why deaf children of deaf parents appear in general to have better developed linguistic skills and to achieve higher academic standards than those deaf children of hearing parents. They also appear to have a much clearer idea of their own identity as a deaf person.

On this premise, hearing parents should understand that inherently, they have all the necessary parenting skills within the context of their family life to bring up and enjoy their deaf child. All help and support should aim to build on and enhance those skills in the most appropriate way for the deaf child in their family.

Issues for the Family

Throughout this chapter the terms family or parent will be used to refer to all those people who are closely related to and involved with the child on a day-to-day basis. This would include parents, single parents, the extended family and indeed any body who could be considered to be in a caring role with the child. These terms will be used interchangeably but if particular people are referred to in this context then their own title will be used.

We accept that it will be the whole family who are affected by having a deaf child and that the impact is not directly on the child itself. The important issue for the child is that the whole family comes to some adjustment to the situation given time and the appropriate support.

We know that the first reactions of hearing parents are likely to be negative, emotional and very strong. They will certainly be in state of shock, followed by denial, grief, anger and guilt. These are symptoms which have been frequently likened to the bereavement process and it is widely accepted that these feelings are perfectly usual for the situation in which parents find themselves.

For example Kath Robinson, who is a hearing mother of a deaf child, describes her initial reaction as she is being given the results of her daughter's hearing test:

> What was deafness? What did it look like? How did it feel? Frantically I searched for some image, a picture of deafness. (Robinson, 1991: 29)

Here are more some reactions taken from personal interviews and from the written experiences of parents when they first find out their child is deaf.

(1) 'When I found out my child was deaf, I cried. I couldn't believe it. I was angry too but I didn't know who with.'
(2) 'I needed a little time just to let the news sink in.'
(3) 'I asked all these question and then I didn't hear the answers'.
(4) 'I remember clearly the absolute devastation.'
(5) 'I thought it would help to meet other deaf mums.'
(6) 'I wanted someone to chat to who knew about deafness.'
(7) 'I saw little girls chattering and thought my daughter will never do that. I didn't think she would ever learn to talk.'
(8) 'How am I going to talk to my child?'
(9) 'I thought it would help to meet another deaf child.'
(10) 'I spent my time crying for what was lost and for not understanding Sophie's problem sooner.'
(11) 'I wanted to know if my child would get married.'
(12) 'I felt I didn't know how to cope with him any more. It all seemed different.' (Sources for this selection: McCracken & Sutherland, 1991; Freeman *et al.*, 1981; Bouvet, 1990)

From these reactions described here, a feel for the type of support and help you as a family may be needing begins to emerge. It appears first that you certainly *need time* — time to allow an assimilation of all the complex feelings and reactions that emerge. You need time and an appreciation from those around you that these feelings are common, natural and the need to express them is totally acceptable.

Secondly it is important for you to find *people to talk to*. Particularly those people who have experienced situations similar to their own and also to people who know about the implications of deafness.

Acquiring *information* is a third factor. There is a wide variety of questions you will want answered. You will want information about a whole range of subjects ranging from educational placement, adult life and what it is like to be deaf. It is interesting that although you will ask a lot of these questions very early on, many parents admit to not really hearing the answer. Lorraine Fletcher who is the parent of a deaf child, comments upon the issue of 'information overload' and the balance between wanting information and the ability to retain it. It seems that parents like to have access to information as and when they want and to select appropriately according to their particular needs at the time.

Fourthly, there are concerns about how you as a family are going to *communicate* with your deaf son or daughter. How are you going to do it and what is the likely outcome for you and your child? It is well appreciated that this can seem an enormous mountain particularly at a time when feelings of stress are running high. It is suggested that hearing parents have:

> An awesome and unusual challenge of raising a child who experiences the world in a way profoundly different from their own experience of the world. Erting (1992: 36)

How can families best be supported during this time of adjustment? From consideration of family reactions to the situation, the needs of most families can be summed up under the following headings. Time to adjust, people to talk to, access to information and help with developing communication with their child. They also need to know what they can actually do in the situation to help them and their child.

Having emphasised that the major adjustment is for the family and that they have needs that certainly deserve attention, nevertheless consideration must be given to the deaf child and the family environment into which they have been born.

Issues for the Child

Having considered some of the likely reactions of the wider family, what are the needs of deaf children specifically? It is simplistic and tempting here to say that the needs of the young deaf baby or child equate with those of any hearing baby or child. After all deaf children are just children who cannot hear, but they do have a normal range of intelligence and need the same opportunities to play and to learn, to grow up and become well functioning adults in the wider society in which they live.

When considering the needs of deaf babies of deaf parents, their needs in the context of social and emotional, physical, cognitive and linguistic development are no different from those of a hearing child. The needs of deaf children will be met naturally within the context of 'good parenting' and 'natural family life' in a home where the significant factor is that the deaf child and their parents share a common language: the sign language of their community.

If deafness is considered from this perspective it can be seen that it is not the deafness itself which gives rise to a special concern but it is the crucial fact that 90% of deaf children have hearing parents. The significance of this is that those very deaf children, for whom sign language will be the emerging preferred mode of communication, are born into an environment where their preferred first language is not the language used at home. The implication for these children, in relation to their need to communicate, is clear.

This need is for them to have the opportunity to develop their linguistic skills at age-appropriate times and to be able to interact meaningfully with their parents, their siblings their peers and with the wider community. The implications here are for parents and the wider family to establish a mode of communication which is appropriate for them and for their particular child's needs. Erting (1997) stresses that the specific needs of deaf, potentially sign language using children of hearing parents are that they are emotionally connected to their parents and develop fluent communication with them.

There are also those less severely deaf children for whom spoken English will be their preferred way of communicating and they will also have clear needs. Their spoken language development is likely to be delayed because of their deafness. This is because although social interaction between parents and their deaf baby will be in spoken English, it is likely to be less natural and intuitive than it would have been with a hearing baby. This is very understandable as most hearing parents become unsure about how to talk to their baby or child when they realise that they cannot be heard well. But nevertheless, the need for those children is also to ensure that their linguistic skills develop at a rate appropriate to their age.

There are two significant points that arise from this discussion of deaf children's linguistic needs. Firstly there is a common need for deaf children of hearing parents to have age-appropriate language development, whether the child's potential communication will be in sign language or spoken English. Secondly, this linguistic need is best met by parents in the home environment, because it is a well established fact that parents have a central, important and an ongoing role in the language development of their children.

The implication of these two complementary issues is that while we know that parents are the most appropriate people to foster that development in their own children, this is the time parents are likely to be in need of support themselves. They need time and the opportunity to develop their own skills and the confidence to bring up and enjoy their own deaf child. So the needs of the child therefore are best met within the family setting with appropriate support and parents should feel reassured that most of what they need to 'know and do' is there within normal parenting skills and that it is possible for other new skills to be learnt and absorbed into the parenting role.

Nature of Support for Families

There has been a history of early intervention and support to the families of deaf children. It has long been recognised that the sooner deafness is diagnosed and appropriate information and help given to parents the more successful are the outcomes for the family. For the majority of hearing families who have deaf children, it is usually a happening outside their everyday experiences. As the diagnosis of deafness is largely a medical matter, families are immediately part of a system where there will initially be doctors, nurses and audiologists involved. Then, rapidly, the local education authority in the guise of teachers and educational psychologists become involved as do social workers and deaf professionals. While all these people have a positive and a constructive role to play, it is important that parents who will be coping with their own emotions and confusions, are not overwhelmed by this wide range of professionals appearing in their lives.

There are many examples of parents feeling that, despite the availability of information and support, somehow they perceive that they have had a lack of information and support, particularly around the time of diagnosis and immediately afterwards. It has been suggested that at that highly emotional time for the family it is difficult to get the support 'right'. Families, and indeed individual parents, seem to have very specific needs at that time. In later discussion with parents it is often clear that one family's idea of help and support or even 'a lifeline' is completely different from that of other families.

What seems to be important is that families should be aware of the range of possible available support and that families can draw from this support that which best meets their own needs.

So when teachers of the deaf, and others, consider the structure and nature of support for families, this should be done in conjunction with the wishes and needs of parents. The following are some of the areas needing joint thought.

Specific needs of each family

Deaf children are born across the whole spectrum of cultural situations. Ethnicity, home language, social and economic status as well as the hearing status of the parents all play their part in affecting the response to deafness in the family. The nuclear family of mother, father and children is no longer automatically the norm. There are many families where both parents work. There are also many lone-parent families who may or may not have the support of an extended family around them. These are additional factors which provide the diversity of backgrounds from which families may come. It is also important to acknowledge that, even within this diverse situation, each family unit will have its own dynamics and family behaviours. This is affected by each individual member's own past experiences and current expectations of family life. Within the family setting each will have their own particular needs and ways of addressing those needs.

Support to families and early-years education programmes must available but should be sensitively planned to allow individualised family support programmes to be developed and implemented.

Hearing parents

Most deaf children are born to hearing parents who have little acquaintance with deaf people and consequently have little or no knowledge of deafness or the deaf community. This is often quoted but does need frequent reiteration, not because we forget the fact but because it is important to remember that each new family has to address this issue afresh. They are usually entering into an area of life which has hitherto been unknown to them. Although there is an accumulated body of knowledge around the impact of deafness on a family, nevertheless for each individual family it is a process which inevitably has to start from the beginning and develop in its own unique way.

Deaf adults will play an important and vital part in the deaf child's life both as a role model and as a sign language user. Some unease has been expressed by hearing families that this link with deaf adults and implicitly with the deaf community will lead to a situation where they feel their deaf child may be 'lost' to the deaf community. They may not be in their rightful place as a member of the family into which they were born. Indeed deaf children using sign language will have an access to the deaf community which may be difficult for hearing adults to replicate. However, there seems to be no real evidence that deaf children are any less close to or part of their hearing family because of their links with the deaf community. They do continue to identify themselves primarily with their family of origin. When parents can recognise their child's deafness and their possible future place within the deaf community as a consequence of this, the perceived threat to the hearing family is reduced.

Families with deaf and hearing members

The practice of always viewing the 'deaf child as member of a hearing family' is potentially a negative concept. David Moores in 1993 high-lighted the fact that the birth of any child into a family fundamentally changes the nature of the family. It means fthat the family has to move into a new stage of adjustment and there will be a disruption to the previous family routine whether it be the first or an additional member. The advent of a deaf child into the family similarly automatically changes the nature of the family. By continuing to view them as a hearing family with a deaf child, the implication is that the child is different and potentially an outsider rather than an integrated member of the family. By definition the family is no longer a hearing family. It becomes a family with both deaf and hearing members. There is an additional element to the family but the family unit as a base for growth and development remains the same. There will be an adjustment in hearing parent's perceptions of the child within the family setting. Also, by understanding that the family can be greatly enriched by the experiences a deaf child can bring means that this identity as family with both deaf and hearing members becomes a positive reality.

Support is a whole family issue

Within the dynamics of the family situation, it is often the mother who becomes primarily involved in the day-to-day caring and support of the deaf child. This can involve hospital visits, meetings with professionals and a variety of other commitments.

While this may be very satisfying and, at one level, very helpful, it can also create a burden for the mother. It means that, in effect, the mother will become the recipient of all information and experience and the family comes to look on her as the fount of knowledge and information. This can put an enormous pressure on her both to have understood and absorbed the vast amount of information open to her and also to be able to transmit it to a wide variety of other people.

In addition it is often the mother who , because she is often the primary carer, becomes the most effective communicator their child and the person who can most easily understand and be understood by their child. This can have an enormous effect on the nature of her relationship with her child. It places her in the role of interpreter in many situations where instead of being able to develop her position as a mother she becomes the child's intermediary. This may not only be in social situations, but also in more quiet, relaxed situations such as watching television, where mother may find she again becomes interpreter. The result of these two factors, where mothers are the source of information and also the most effective communicator, is that they may be carrying a heavy and disproportionate burden in the context of the whole family.

Support should have built-in flexibility to ensure that information is as accessible to fathers and other members of the family as it is to mothers. Similarly discussions about communication options should be available to everyone as should the choice for all members of the family to learn sign language if this is appropriate. This means that professionals should be prepared to meet families at times convenient for them and that also employers should be sensitive to the needs of their employees in allowing time off work to allow fathers to have an equal share in the care and upbringing of their deaf child.

By ensuring that information and support is open to the whole family, by implication the responsibility for the deaf child becomes a whole family issue involving siblings, parents and grandparents on an equal and relevant footing. This gives the child the opportunity to move appropriately, naturally and freely, from their initial affiliation to their primary-care giver, usually their mother, to a broader relationship with their father and siblings and the wider family. Communication becomes a whole family issue where all members are encouraged to develop a mode of communication that is successful with the child. This not only partly frees the mother from a burdensome role with the child and the rest of the family but also encourages within the child a proactive and independent role in developing their own receptive and expressive communicative skills.

Changing needs

As the parents' attitude to their child's deafness changes so will their needs in terms of support change. The needs of a family at the time of identification of a hearing loss, and then at diagnosis, have already been explored in this chapter. They are best met by reflecting the individual needs of the family. The aims of support are that the family should make a smooth and constructive adjustment to the fact that they are now a family with deaf and hearing members and that their child's natural development is not interrupted by the needs of a family who were expecting a hearing child.

As the child develops and the needs change, then the pressures on the family will also change and again the type of support needs to reflect that. In common with all families, the time when their child enters formal education is critical. Most deaf children will have had pre-school and nursery experience, but somehow the start of formal education is a big step. It involves parents letting go of some of their responsibilities. Often entering school requires the model of support available to change from the largely family-centred pre-school support to a more child-focused, school-based model. Despite family support groups organised within the school situation, this can lead to the family feeling isolated from their child, and their knowledge of the day-to-day activities is drastically reduced. If their child is placed in school some distance from home then inevitably there may have to be a taxi or a bus journey to school, the idea of which can be very upsetting to parents.

Similarly entry into adolescence and later adulthood can bring their own special tensions into the family situation. What is clear is that while families are usually supported through the initial adjustment time, parents of deaf children do face continuing tensions and stresses and are required to go on facing changing situations and the expectation that they will adjust accordingly.

Respect for the reality of deafness

It is important for families to understand that deafness as a state is largely unchangeable and currently cannot be 'cured'. For some parents, a way of coping with their stress is to satisfy themselves that they have explored every possible avenue to ameliorate or 'cure' the situation. We know it is important for the child to have appropriate amplification, the correct educational programmes and any prescribed medical therapy. It is also important that parents should understand what is a positive and constructive way to proceed and what may be unproductive and lead only to a feeling of frustration for themselves and of insecurity for their child. It is important for the self-image of the child, for parents to focus clearly and positively on what the child can do and the language they can develop and not always on their hearing loss and difficulties with spoken language.

It appears that this 'seeking a cure' approach of some parents may be less prevalent when parents are encouraged to consider a linguistic rather than a medical framework (as discussed in Chapter 2) for viewing their child's deafness. Support and advice to parents should encourage them to see deafness not as a tragedy but to concentrate on the many positive attributes their child has for them immediately. It is not possible for any professional to predict exactly how a child will develop either socially or linguistically. It is possible for all deaf children to develop communication, be it spoken or sign language, with their families and with the wider community and that they and all the family will lead a fuller and richer life because of it.

Types of support

Support for deaf families comes from three main sources. First it comes from other families of deaf children who have already experienced the sort of emotions and feelings that a family of a newly diagnosed deaf child may be feeling. They are the only people who can truly share and understand the situation and say 'Yes we do know what it feels like' ... 'Yes I do know what you mean' ... 'We know exactly why you are saying that' ... 'I understand why you are saying that'. These are families who are in the same situation but at different stages along the track. This gives parents the opportunity to meet deaf children of all ages, some still at home, some at school, some in nursery; all bright and sociable children developing their communication skills with their parents and other children. It is important that all the family, including grandparents and siblings, meet other families and their children where the fear of the unknown, that is the deaf child, can be dispersed and put into perspective. Families will have that very real practical assurance that their baby will develop and become a happy child who will play, go to school, ride a bike, possibly become a moody teenager and very likely get married as most deaf people do.

Second, meeting with deaf children, deaf adults and members of the deaf community is a vital source of support for all deaf children and their families. They are all models for deaf children and their families — as adults and children living full and busy lives. They are the source of the full and rich language which will become the first language for many deaf children and a second language for other deaf children. Their understanding of, and rapport with deaf children, and their visual/gestural communication skills are a rich source for both children and families alike and their value cannot be underestimated. The parenting process for both deaf and hearing families is common in many ways. The specific linguistic and parenting skills of deaf adults are an additional sources of expertise which complement those of hearing parents and become a valuable source of skills for hearing parents to absorb.

Third, a wide variety of professionals, for example, teachers of the deaf, social workers, educational psychologists and audiologists will become involved with deaf children and their families and they all have different areas of expertise which will be of value to the family at varying times. It is important for parents to meet all professionals involved early on and to understand their role within the support team. Parents can then decide for themselves when and who they would like to be in contact with. It is likely that the first person the family will come into contact with, apart from hospital personnel in the form of doctors, nurses and audiologists, will be an advisory teacher of the deaf. They will be working as part of a team involving social workers for deaf people, educational psychologists as well deaf adults Their role becomes central to the support offered and they are considered to have a key role with the family. To avoid an excess of professionals involved with the family it is suggested that each family has a named person to coordinate the support offered to the family. The nature of support from these professionals is mainly in the form of information imparting in the areas of communication, educational choices and placement, and in guidance through the complications of the educational system. It is important that parents understand the value of people around them who have wide experience and knowledge in all aspects and implications of deafness.

Full and balanced information

Access to full and balanced information is a family's right and there is a responsibility on the teacher of the deaf to ensure that the family has that access. However, there is a skill in imparting information at the right time, in the right terms and depth to avoid that common complaint of parents, that they are suffering from 'information overload'. This can provide a dilemma for the teacher who is obliged to ensure that full information is given but must accept that much of what they are saying will need reiterating at another time. The common aim for both parents and teachers should be that the support from the teachers will ensure that the information and guidance they are offering is in direct response to parental need. Through the parents' growing knowledge of deafness and their own child they should grow in confidence and become empowered to make their own informed decisions about their child and their child's future. Parents should trust and be trusted to know their children better than anyone else. It is this fact combined with their access to full and balanced information which means that they can then become equal partners with the professionals with whom they come into contact. Thus any decisions are made in the light of full knowledge and in conjunction with professions.

Child's role in developing communication

Deaf children have a role in developing their most appropriate mode of communication. We accept that support to all families will come from both deaf and hearing families and professionals and from this experience deaf children will be exposed to both spoken and signed languages. The child will be exposed to a range of communication options in the natural course of their lives, that is sign language from interaction with deaf adults and children and spoken English in the wider community. This means that parents do not have to make impossibly difficult decisions about their baby on very little knowledge or evidence of their child's particular aptitude for language. They have time then to develop their own communicative skills with their child in the knowledge that their child has access at the same time to good models of both signed and spoken languages. This scenario allows the child's own predisposition for their preferred language to emerge and for the children themselves to guide parents and teachers along their own preferred linguistic route.

Parents should be parents

Deaf children need parents who are functioning in their traditional role as parents. Natural parenting does have an implicit teaching aspect in the areas of language, social and cognitive development. However to feel the need to take on a more conscious and explicit teaching role can drastically interfere with the parenting role. What parents can do is to transfer what they do learn from the child's teacher, from deaf people and from other parents to the home situation and there create an environment which is conducive to learning and living a full and exciting life.

All support should aim to enable parents to function fully and enjoy their rightful and proper role as parents. To this end, support should ensure that parents do not feel alone and worried and that they do develop a relaxed form of communication with their child. For this to happen, they and their child need access to a wide circle of support and easy opportunities to interact with other deaf and hearing families. These opportunities can be provided partly through educational and medical support and through parent support groups and voluntary organisations. Access to this type of support should relieve parents of the pressure to become teacher, interpreter and communicator for their child and instead allow them to take up, concentrate on and enjoy their irreplaceable role as parents.

Conclusion

Personal experience of working with the families of deaf children would confirm the following quotation:

> Despite the very real problems of communication, understanding and acceptance most deaf children and their families apparently make better adjustments than they have been credited for. (Moores, 1996: 148)

In the opening words of this chapter, it is emphasised that in no way should the profound effect a deaf child can have on a family be minimised. In general parents and families are able to move away from the expectations they would have had for the hearing child they were awaiting and to go some way towards accepting deafness as a lifelong part of their family's life. That successful deaf children grow up to be successful deaf adults is living proof that most families are able to make this adjustment.

Summary

For all hearing families the addition of a deaf son or daughter to their household will be a life-changing experience. They have changed from a hearing family to one with both deaf and hearing members. In the early days of adjustment it is important that the needs of the family are respected as well as the needs of the deaf child. This is the time when various professional people are likely to become involved with the family offering support and information. They need to be aware that each family is an individual unit and the support needs to be planned accordingly. However, all support should appreciate that most families need:

- time to adjust,
- people to talk to,
- access to information,
- help with developing communication with their child.

Additional Reading

Fletcher, L. (1987) *Language for Ben*. London: Souvenir Press.
This book is written by the mother of a deaf child and reflects her reactions to the deafness in her son Ben and her family's subsequent journey to establish effective communication and education for him.

Mahshie, S. (1995) *Educating Deaf Children Bilingually*. Washington, D.C.: Gallaudet University Press.
Chapter 3 describes family reactions and all aspects of the family's involement with the development of deaf children.

Erting, C. (1992) Partnership for change: Creating new worlds for deaf children and their families. In *Bilingual Considerations in the Education of Deaf Students* (ASI and English Gallaudet University Conference Proceedings). Washington, DC: Gallaudet University Press.
This conference paper considers carefully the needs of families of deaf children as well as the needs of the children themselves.

Chapter 4

Home and the Wider World

Introduction

Deaf children are likely to experience the world in ways that are different from their hearing peers. While hearing children experience the world through their hearing, and are so part of an 'auditory' culture, deaf children are visual beings and are part of a 'visual' culture. This difference is most obvious in the area of communication. It is also true that, in many ways, deaf children encounter the world in a different way from their hearing friends This may be from their immediate response from the family to experiences of hospital, education and the wider community. This chapter aims to discuss some of these 'different' experiences and then to explore the family and deaf child's possible responses to them.

The Deaf Child

A deaf child is just like a hearing child except they cannot hear. This is a phrase which is often heard and is easy to repeat. It is simplistic, misleading and does not do justice to or show respect for either deaf or hearing children. Consider two newly born babies, one deaf and one hearing, where there are no additional difficulties for either. Apart from this one biological difference, the opening statement in this paragraph could be true. Biologically the two children could be very similar.

At this point it seems appropriate to bring in some introductory theory about child development so that we can think further about deaf and hearing children's development. At the moment current thinking strongly suggests that both biological factors (those you are born with) and the environmental factors (those you experience) affect the development of all children, hearing or deaf. This is commonly known as the nature/nurture theory. There is still an area of debate about the degree to which each of these factors affects this development. Environmentalists argue that the experience a child has of the world affects their development more strongly, while others favour the idea that biological factors dictate more strongly how a person's cognitive and intellectual development will unfold. A more general view would suggest that both factors influence the development of a person to a greater or lesser degree depending upon the individual child and that the two factors work together and are not separate influences.

Wherever one chooses to stand in this debate, the fact is that deaf children are born with one major sense (i.e. hearing) affected and do not access the sounds of the environment as hearing children do. Because of this, deaf children experience the world in a different way from their hearing peers and siblings. Carol Erting (1992: 36) described this difference in perception of the world as:

> hearing children living in an auditory and visual world whereas a deaf child experiences the world primarily through vision.

These two factors together suggest that the language and the related cognitive development of deaf children is likely to be different from that of hearing children. This is not to suggest that it is inferior in any way, but it should be accepted that it will be different. How this different experience of the world may influence the deaf child's development will be explored later in this chapter.

This 'different' experience will also have an effect on a deaf child's language development. This can happen in two ways. It is now thought that, from the very early stages, a child's language development is a two-way process and the child, however small, is as much a part of that interaction as their parents. It depends as much on the child's response as it does on the parent's input. If the adult's input is unsure and the child's responses unclear, then its early experience of interaction will be different. This 'unsure' interaction is often the situation for young deaf children. It is particularly true for those deaf children born to hearing parents where the best way to communicate is not clear early on.

The second relevant theory is that it is children's ability with language which affects the way in which they understand and endeavour to make sense of the world around them and the people in it. In other words it is children themselves have an affect on how the world responds to them. This means that if their perception of the world is different, then 'the world' will respond in correspondingly different ways. While this is true for all children, it is particularly relevant for those children whose language may be developing in a different modality from their family and the wider society.

So it is understood that deaf children's perceptions and experiences of the world and of interaction will be different from hearing children. It is interesting for us to explore how they may experience the world and how these experiences affect the way their cognitive and linguistic skills develop.

It is important to restate that there is nothing to suggest that the biological state of deafness (that is an inability for whatever reason, to access sounds in the way a hearing person can) in itself affects the linguistic and cognitive potential of that child. Just because a person cannot hear the sounds of speech it does not follow that they are not capable of developing a language and their intellect. What it does mean is that the usual channel for developing these linguistic and cognitive skills, that is access to language and environmental sounds through hearing, is partly or wholly reduced. So the challenge for families of deaf children and the people supporting them is to find ways of communicating with their children which will ensure that their experience of the world is positive and appropriate.

The next part of this chapter will look at how young deaf children appear to experience the world and the issues to be considered in relation to their cognitive, linguistic and social development. We know that all these areas of development are interlinked and interdependent and are a reflection of the child's language competence and experience of the wider world.

Experiences in the Family

We have said before that many aspects of the deaf child's experiences within the family and their wider world will be different from that of a hearing child and that this is not a negative experience in itself. The suggestion is that if we have a greater understanding of how the deaf child experiences the world then we will know more about how these different experiences may influence a child's development.

A child's development must be set into context. That is, it is important to understand that it is part of a process which starts before their birth, considers the family and social setting into which they are born, continues through school and adolescence into adulthood. Throughout that lifespan the family, the wider society and other institutions will have an ongoing and variable influence depending upon the situation.

To explore the environment as experienced by deaf children we need to move the focus of attention to the 'significant people' who influence and affect the deaf child's world. Significant people begin with the child's immediate family, extending to the wider family, friends, teachers and members of the wider community who become involved with the family.

It is clear that the immediate family of the deaf child has issues to face and decisions to make that will mean that some aspects of family life may well be different. A previous chapter explored the reactions of parents to the diagnosis of deafness in a young child. At that sensitive time, parents are also confronted with many decisions to be made but the most crucial and far reaching is about the mode of communication they will adopt with their deaf child (this is more fully described in Chapter 5). Whichever mode is adopted, there will be implications for all the family.

Experiences of Communication

For parents who decide to use sign language with their deaf child, there are implications for all family members including brothers, sisters and grandparents. It is implicit that many family members will undertake to learn sign language. However, it is often the case that mothers become the most efficient communicators with their deaf child. This is understandable, because of the nature of their day-to-day contact with their child. This does, however, have implications for the mothering role. (It is important to realise that it is not necessarily the mother who takes this role. The following would apply to whoever becomes the principal caretaker of the child. For convenience we will continue to use the term 'mother' to represent the principal carer of the child.)

As the child develops, the mother may find herself in the role of interpreter both for conversations within the home as well as for television programmes, and become the major channel for communication for their child and the wider world. Not only can this put a burden on her but fathers often feel a bit excluded from communicating with their own child through lack of well developed sign language skills. It is a good idea for mothers to be aware of their changing role with the child and to 'back off' occasionally from being the interpreter and let other family members develop their own skills and strategies.

It has been observed that left to their own devices, children and grandparents, aunts and uncles can usually manage to make themselves understood if they are encouraged to do so. While consistency in languages within the family should be encouraged to allow the deaf child the opportunity experience a consistent input, it is also important for all family members to establish their own particular skills and to develop their own relationship with the children in the usual way.

Although all parents are always, in part, teachers of their own children, it is mostly an incidental role within the context of everyday family life. With a deaf child there is often felt to be a need for this teaching role to become more explicit. Families often feel expected to provide more specific 'teaching' of language leading to them feeling they should have a conscious and active teaching role. Sometimes this can conflict with their role as parents and interfere with relaxed play and mutual enjoyment. If parents do feel they should do some 'teaching' then it should be for short periods of 'quality time' and the rest should be time as parents.

Some families become overwhelmed and so engrossed in the deafness of their child that other aspects of family life become lost. This may be time which needs to be given to other members of the family such as brothers and sisters. If they feel they are being neglected at the expense of their deaf sibling then, not only will their relationships suffer, but the whole balance of family life can be altered.

Often hearing parents feel particularly protective towards their deaf children, usually when communication is not well developed, and they fear that the child cannot understand for themselves the limitations and dangers that are around. Similarly parents often make concessions for their deaf children and accept patterns of behaviour they would not accept in hearing siblings, overlooking bed times and rules which would apply to other members of the family.

All these situations can subtly affect the balance and dynamics of family life. An awareness of them can, in some cases, minimise the negative effects. An acceptance that the dynamics of the family are changed by the presence of a deaf child is crucial and a perception of the family as one which now has with both deaf and hearing members is helpful in adjusting to the changes. It must be remembered that it is as important for the deaf child to come to terms with being deaf in a hearing world as it is for parents to adjust to their deafness.

Experiences of Education

Young deaf children's experiences of 'education' starts much earlier than for most hearing children. Support to the family is offered from the time of diagnosis of deafness. As part of the support team, there is likely to be a teacher of the deaf whose role it is to offer support and guidance to the family. This teacher will usually visit the family at home and be involved in decisions about choice of communication within the family and also encourage the family to provide a stimulating and appropriate home environment for the deaf child. It is important that this advice and support is not overwhelming to a family who may not yet be ready to deal with all the advice they receive. There are education programmes offered by speech therapy clinics and support and language groups run by education authorities. While all these activities are certainly valuable, it may be at the price of less time spent in a relaxed home environment within the normal family setting. Such attention to explicit teaching and language input is certainly unusual at such an early age as is regular attendance at clinics and support groups.

Deaf children often enter formal school education programmes earlier than their hearing peers. It is not unusual for nursery or kindergarten places to be offered to children as young as two. While the value of these placements, both for linguistic and social development, is not to be underestimated, it is nevertheless unusual for the formal education of children to begin at such an early age.

Both in nursery, primary and secondary school, deaf children often form more intensive relationships with their teachers than do their hearing friends. This is because there is likely to be a much lower staff/child ratio for deaf children and teachers of the deaf support children throughout a longer period of their school life than many teachers. Communication plays a significant part in teacher–pupil relationships. Often it is the teachers of the deaf who are better able to communicate with deaf children than the hearing staff or peer group. This can lead to teachers and other school personnel having a particularly profound influence upon the development of deaf children. One of the things teachers should be aware of in this close relationship is that they should make sure that deaf children also learn independence both with their friends and in the classroom.

Families may be faced with decisions about appropriate educational placements for their children. There is the choice between integrated and segregated educational establishments and those with different communication modes. Occasionally, and particularly in more rural areas, parents are faced with the possibility of their children attending a residential school. These are choices and decisions which do not usually affect the families of hearing children.

Experience of the Wider World

The community in which a deaf child lives has a profound influence on the child. In the case of deaf children, they are faced with two possible communities: the wider hearing community and the deaf community. These influences will vary depending upon their family situation and the attitudes of those closest to them. Some deaf children have easy access to the ideas and attitudes of the deaf community through the family's link with deaf adults. For others such ideas are filtered through family and professionals. Aspects of the deaf community of which children may quickly become aware are the function and place of the deaf clubs in the deaf person's life as both a social setting and as a support network. There are subtitling and signed programmes on the television and more books for children are appearing with sign graphics and finger spelling representation of the text.

The most important and visual influence of the deaf community for the deaf child is exposure to sign language. For the majority of deaf children with hearing parents, their mixing with the deaf community takes place outside the home. This means that, as their sign language skills develop, the majority of their socialising takes place with people other than their parents. This is an important feature in the development of deaf children: the acceptance that the immediate family may not be the centre of their social life.

The hearing community generally has little immediate knowledge or understanding of deafness and deaf people. Therefore, when a deaf child is born into a hearing family, friends and neighbours will often find it difficult to respond to a deaf child in a relaxed and natural way. This means that the deaf child may not have the opportunity of relaxed early interaction with members of their wider world. It has been suggested by some parents that friends and relations avoid contact because they are both embarrassed and uncomfortable and do not know how to approach the situation appropriately. It often falls to parents to enable other hearing people to feel comfortable in the situation.

One of the features of deafness affecting the response of the hearing community is the initial 'invisible' nature of deafness. In this way deafness is different from other disabilities and it is not until the deaf child begins to develop specific coping strategies for interaction with other people that their deafness becomes noticeable.

Deafness becomes a recognisable condition through such channels as the wearing of hearing aids, the development of speech which may not be well articulated and the use of sign language. It is how the hearing community responds to these outward signs of deafness, and how the child interprets these, that affects how they respond to and cope with the hearing world. The response to hearing aids is often that other hearing people assume that now the deaf child can hear as a hearing child does. Another response to seeing the hearing aid is to shout or to over enunciate words.

These likely approaches can be disconcerting for the deaf child as the very act of shouting affects a person's facial appearance and can easily be interpreted as anger or displeasure. Over enunciation of words again leads to inappropriate lip patterns and distortion of facial features. Both of these factors can be at best confusing for a deaf child and at worst, upsetting and again it falls to the parents to enlighten hearing people who often make assumptions about how best to interact with deaf children through a lack of knowledge about and unfamiliarity with deafness and deaf children. It can be a hard task for parents who are often coming to terms with these issues themselves to also become advocates for their own children. As the young deaf child begins to articulate, his or her speech sounds are often ill formed and difficult to understand. Again this 'lack of success' with interaction means that deaf children do not always have comfortable interactions with those people who know them less well.

The use of sign language similarly can inhibit relaxed interaction with hearing people who are at loss to respond to the child's possible initiations. Hearing people should be encouraged to relax and persevere in their relationships with deaf children and their family, as it is through these everyday encounters with the hearing friends and relations that deaf children begin to develop strategies of their own for living in the wider hearing community.

In conclusion, there has been research into the overall development of deaf children in relation to the 'different experience' that they are perceived to have of the world. In some cases, parents with no experience of deafness do tend to be more restrictive of their children's social and physical experiences. While this may have some effect on the child's confidence and development, there is no evidence to suggest that the condition of deafness *per se* affects their development. Sometimes the inappropriate response to deafness from the wider community can have an effect.

The Deaf Child's Development

If the deaf child's development is to be fully understood, it must be set in the context of the child's environment. An awareness of the way in which many deaf children are presented with a different model of the world is important in understanding their responses to the wider community in which they live and the influence this may have on their responses to it.

Social development

Deaf children who are involved with their families in early support programmes generally are better adjusted socially than those who have not had that experience. Appropriate support can help parents adjust to having a deaf child in the family, and the opportunity to meet other families and children offers valuable mutual support. Commitment to being within a support programme would indicate significant and important parental involvement with their children's deafness and with their education. Also, the language training available for parents and children within such support groups provides a setting for parent/child communication which reflects their linguistic as well as their social development. Continued opportunity for interaction with deaf and hearing peers and adults in the nursery and school settings gives the opportunity for the further development of children's social skills.

Language development

It is accepted that the rate of deaf children's language development is affected by their degree of deafness, the language of the home into which they are born, their early linguistic experiences and their own desire to communicate. It is known that learning a language is a two-way process. It develops through interaction between the child and a person with well-developed language skills. For deaf children of deaf parents, where the language of the home is immediately compatible with the needs of the deaf child, that child is likely to develop language at an age equivalent to that of hearing children. This is because they share a common language and interaction is natural and relaxed from the time of birth.

For hearing parents decisions are not so easy. Because we know that deaf children of deaf parents can and do develop language age-appropriately, then we know that it is not deafness itself which affects the speed of language development, but it is the opportunity for deaf children to access and therefore learn a language that is problematic. It is important for parents to appreciate the needs of their children and to develop the appropriate skills to communicate in a relaxed and productive way.

Development of intelligence and learning skills

Available evidence suggests that the condition of deafness itself poses no limitations on the cognitive and learning potential of deaf children. They have the same range of intelligence as hearing children and their ways of thinking are no less sophisticated. Deaf children apparently address problems in much the same way as hearing children. The fact that sometimes deaf children do less well in tests and in some academic subjects is more likely to be because of a lack of understanding of the test materials and subject matter than in their ability to learn. We know that some areas of deaf children's intelligence are more developed and others are less so than hearing children. (There is further discussion of this in Chapter 10.) Because we know that deaf children of deaf parents generally achieve their academic potential especially those in mainstream school, then it is likely that their more natural language development has had an effect on this. It is considered that language development and cognitive development are linked in many ways, and this reiterates the importance of families developing a comfortable and appropriate way of communicating with their child.

The Young Deaf Person

Childhood and adolescence are a time of growth and development as social skills develop and the child's personality begins to emerge. This takes place through interaction with the family and other children in the home, the school and other social settings. This pattern of behaviour is the same for both deaf and hearing children where they look for, and need, the same emotional and practical everyday support, are influenced by the same external factors and develop the same kinds of behaviours. Deaf children can be equally well adjusted in their behaviour as their hearing peers.

However, poor communication with family and friends may cause some deaf children and adolescents to receive less explicit explanations, and so be less aware of social rules, than hearing children. This can lead to a slower development of self-esteem and independence. Some of the conflicting emotions in adolescence are a result of striving to find our own self-esteem and self-identity.

As deaf and hearing children move towards the secondary school, the school and their school friends become more important social influences than their families. The values of school and peers becomes much more influential. Deaf children have to cope with and learn to deal with the same social issues as hearing children. As both deaf and hearing children become older, brothers and sisters, peers and adults outside the home become more influential and it is now in this setting that social rules and social behaviour are affected.

As the young deaf person leaves school for college or work their transition will be affected by both their educational attainments as well as other social factors. This period of transition from child to adult or from school to the world of work or college is primarily one of growing independence from the family. This is a period of great adjustment for both children and for the family. The family who had become used to their young deaf child now have to recognise their son or daughter as a deaf adult. This is a hard transition for families of hearing children as well as those of deaf children.

Conclusion

Complex issues are faced by hearing parents with deaf children. As the family moves through different life stages, different strains are placed on them. Despite these real problems of communication, understanding and acceptance, most families do make better adjustments than often credited (Moores, 1996). Without minimising the profound impact of a deaf child on the family, most families do accommodate, at least to some degree, the implications of deafness within their family. The general success of their children makes it clear that despite their feelings, most parents do go a long way towards this by developing productive forms of communication to suit their children, by enjoying their children and developing into a family with both deaf and hearing members.

Summary

This chapter has taken the stance that deaf children do indeed experience the world in ways that are different from their hearing peers and friends. Much of this difference is related to issues to do with linguistic mode and competence within that mode. The chapter encourages parents to become aware of these issues and to appreciate that they do not adversely affect deaf children's development. They do contribute to the fact that deaf children may well develop specific strategies for communicating and for learning. The major influences in these areas are as follows:

- experiences in the family,
- experiences of communication,
- experiences of education,
- experiences of the wider world.

This development is ongoing and affects their development through from childhood to adolescence and adulthood

Additional Reading

Meadows-Orlans, K. (1990) Research on developmental aspects of deafness. In D. Moores and K. Meadows-Orlans (eds) *Educational and Developmental Aspects of Deafness*. Washington, DC: Gallaudet University Press.
    This chapter considers in more depth the issues related to the development of deaf children.

Marschark, M. (1997) *Raising and Educating a Deaf Child*. Oxford: Oxford University Press.
    Chapter 5 looks, in particular, at the language development of deaf children.

Chapter 5
Language Choices at Home

Introduction

The central concern for all deaf children and their parents is the successful establishment of language and communication skills. Such skills are important for almost every aspect of life. To know a language, whether it be a spoken or a signed language, enables us to communicate our needs, ideas and emotions to each other and to define ourselves as individuals within our social world. As the parent of a deaf child you will probably have given a great deal of thought to your child's language development and probably have realised that there is no one straightforward route for any family. All deaf children are individuals with diverse communication needs and this is reflected in the different ways in which families with deaf members choose to communicate between themselves.

For some deaf children, spoken language may be sufficiently accessible with the help of hearing-aid technology. For others, access to spoken language may be more difficult and sign language may be a more appropriate primary language. The identification of individual language and communication need is not clear cut, as most deaf children cannot be grouped simply into a sign language or a spoken language group. To successfully address an individual child's needs at home, we should consider the whole child within the range of situations they are likely to encounter. We will refer to this interaction of linguistic, environmental and social factors as a continuum of language need as this moves away from the tendency to categorise children into two distinct groups according to audiological descriptors. This chapter will identify and describe this range of communication needs in different contexts and, by doing so, explore the role of both spoken and signed languages (and the interaction between them) in the deaf child's home experiences.

What is Communication?

Our knowledge and experience of language is a unique and distinctive human quality which is central to the way in which we construct and organise our experiences and our understanding of the world around us. Language and communication are essential for our cultural, educational and individual social development. We need language for learning; it allows us to think aloud, to rehearse, to memorise and to tackle and make sense of new concepts and new experiences. Language and communication also enable us to socialise, as we develop our interests and our ability to make relationships with those around us. The fundamental needs of deaf children with regard to language and communication skills are little different from those of any developing child.

Communication as a means to an end

Language can be described as the essential bank of knowledge or tools that we use to communicate whereas communication is a means to an end. When we communicate we use our knowledge of language to achieve certain goals and it is this functional aspect of language that this chapter will focus on. In relation to the deaf child's communication needs, the key features of communication which we need to keep in mind are:

- Communication is an essentially **social and interpersonal activity** which allows the sharing of thoughts, meanings and ideas between people
- Communication is a **skilled behaviour** which incorporates the use of a language system as well as the use of certain non-linguistic features such as eye-contact, body posture and gesture.

Communication as a social activity

Because communicating is essentially a social activity, a hearing child will acquire the fundamental skills in communication from early interactive experiences. For many deaf children and their families, the development of successful and positive communication can be a more difficult issue. If we look at some examples of what communication skills involve, it is likely that they are skills we use naturally and that we will not remember being consciously taught them:

- applying our knowledge of language to get the desired result;
- shaping our language or our message to match the knowledge or experience of the audience or listener;
- applying the necessary social skills such as turn-taking, eye-contact, and the use of other non-verbal strategies, such as smiling or nodding;
- identifying the main points of the speaker's message which may be ambiguous or fragmented.

In our exploration of the range of deaf children's communication needs, we will consider both the inter-personal nature of communication as well as the notion of communication as a skilled behaviour which, by implication, can be taught and can be learned. Deafness itself should not be a barrier to successful and easy communication, and there is no reason why deaf children should not become confident communicators given the appropriate support.

Communication goals

All children should have the opportunity to:

- become confident communicators in whichever language is appropriate to the setting and purpose of the interaction;
- be able to use communication as a means to achieving their academic potential and to eventually make choices about the future;
- be able to use communication to successfully develop relationships with peers and make connections with others throughout life;
- be able to make communication choices which feed a positive sense of identity and high level of self-esteem.

Identifying Deaf Children's Communication Needs

To talk about deaf children's individual communication needs the terms preferred language or preferred mode of communication are often used. The use of the word 'preferred' is often greeted with some alarm and confusion as it is frequently misinterpreted as linked with a notion of choice. In this context, the term 'preferred' refers to the language in which a child finds it easier to make an utterance in any area of experience at any given time. When assessing the communicative needs of any deaf child, parents and teachers do not simply wait until a preferred mode of communication emerges, but will make some informed decisions about the nature and extent of the individual's communication needs and how best to address these needs. These decisions will be based on factors such as:

- *The nature and extent of the child's deafness.* Generally, children with a mild-to-moderate loss will experience some difficulty in hearing speech at conversational level, but children with severe or greater deafness are unlikely to be able to perceive speech without amplification.

- *The hearing status of the family and the languages used in the home.* Other family members (parents, siblings, extended family) may be deaf or all the family may be hearing. The language of the home may also be different to that of the majority culture.
- *The child's functional use of spoken English and sign language.* The child may demonstrate skills in either or both languages in different situations. This information may provide an indicator of the child's preferred mode of communication.

These are criteria used by professionals but as a parent you know your child better than anyone and the information you share with professionals about your child's developing language is invaluable.

Case Studies

As a starting point for considering how these factors interact with each other, the two extremes of the continuum of linguistic need will be explored by contrasting the communication needs of two different deaf children. It would be dangerous to assume that all deaf children's needs can be categorised in such a way, but by providing these two cases as a starting point, the range of need can be illustrated.

Matthew — a deaf child for whom spoken language is the preferred language

At one end of the continuum is Matthew, who has a mild loss of 40 dB. The implications of this loss with regard to speech perception are that although he will be able to detect the sounds of conversation, he is likely to miss the sounds of speech which are weakest in intensity such as fricative sounds 'f' and 's' and nasal sounds like 'm' and 'n'. He is also likely to miss endings on words such as plurals and any other unstressed components of speech. The appropriate amplification through hearing aids will not totally restore his hearing but provide him with approximately a 30 dB gain.

Matthew's family are all hearing and English is the home language. Matthew attends his local school where he receives some support from a teacher of the deaf (one visit every two weeks). He has hearing friends in his class who live near him and whom he sees at weekends or after school. His preferred language is spoken English and this is the language of the home. He demonstrates the potential to achieve an age-appropriate level of proficiency in spoken English.

A summary of Matthew's communication needs incorporating home and school would include the following:

- opportunities for meaningful and pleasurable spoken language interaction in the home leading to easy spoken language communication at home which facilitates the practicalities of everyday life;
- an emphasis on access to the full school curriculum through spoken and written English with appropriate visual support and differentiation of materials;
- an emphasis on the development of spoken language skills in the school setting through a programme of focused speech and language work and specific training in the appropriate use and maintenance of both radio and post-aural aids;
- additional support in school for the development of literacy skills through a closely monitored individual programme or scheme of work;
- consideration given in school to an optimum physical environment including good listening conditions, appropriate seating arrangements and classroom sound proofing; and
- opportunities to work and play collaboratively with hearing peers in small groups or one-to-one situations in the school setting and to develop peer friendships in the home context.

Elizabeth — a deaf child for whom sign language is the preferred language

At the other end of the continuum is Elizabeth who has a profound loss of 100+ dB which is progressively deteriorating. The implications of this are that she is likely only to experience limited and often distorted perception of speech sounds even with very powerful amplification, and her perception of sounds varies from day to day. She also suffers from another accompanying feature of sensori-neural deafness known as 'recruitment' which means that she finds small increases in sound painful and difficult to tolerate.

Elizabeth has deaf parents and a deaf older brother. She attends a residential school for the deaf where sign language is recognised as a language and where she is taught by both deaf and hearing adults. Most of her school friends are deaf but when she returns home at weekends and for holidays, she sometimes plays with neighbouring children who are all hearing. Sign language (BSL) is Elizabeth's preferred language in that it is the language of the home, but also the language in which she has the highest level of skills and through which she is able to learn most efficiently.

A summary of Elizabeth's communication needs incorporating home and school would include:

- opportunities for meaningful and pleasurable sign language inter- action in the home setting leading to easy communication at home which facilitates the practicalities of everyday life;
- an emphasis on the development of age-appropriate sign language skills through both exposure to sign language in use as well as direct sign language teaching;
- an emphasis on access to the full school curriculum and assessment through BSL;
- a sustained programme for the development of a high level of skills in English as a second language with emphasis on the development of literacy skills;
- an emphasis on functional strategies for communicating with hearing people and the development of spoken language and listening/watching skills;
- opportunities to develop both deaf and hearing peer friendships in the home context.

These two examples demonstrate how the two key aspects of communi- cation, that is the inter-personal aspects and communication as a skilled behaviour, can both be considered in any assessment of communication need. The needs we have identified for both Matthew and Elizabeth incorporate the importance of maximising opportunities for interaction as well as the need to provide focused programmes of support for the development of specific skills.

You may feel that you recognise either Matthew or Elizabeth or some of their characteristics. However, these two contrasting examples of individual need present two extremes of a continuum which will be further explored in the next section. It must be stressed that children do not usually fall into the tidy categories exemplified by Matthew and Elizabeth. In order to consider a more diverse range of needs, a sample of case studies of different children will be explored with a particular emphasis on the home setting.

Language Choices at Home

The choices that you make about language use to meet these identified needs will depend on the make-up of your individual family. Professional advice is often offered on this issue but most families have to find the most comfortable and successful way of operating for themselves and the

choices made vary tremendously. You may well decide to use predominantly spoken language in the home, perhaps with some sign support
and gesture. Alternatively, you might find your way to a sign language
class as soon as possible and aim to use BSL in the home. In many hearing
families, communication with the deaf child is a combination of sign
language and English. In homes where there are one or two deaf parents,
more sign language may be used but we cannot assume that all deaf
parents prefer to use sign language as some of the case studies will
illustrate.

Generally parents and children are both resourceful and creative in
their approach to making communication work for the family, and their
way of operating is intuitive and pragmatic rather than based on formal
decisions. We will see through the case studies how in the home setting,
different modes of communication may be used for different purposes at
different times with different people.

Meeting the communication needs of the deaf child in the home setting
involves addressing the following issues:

- the need for the child to develop positive relationships with parents
  and siblings and the extended family by being able to communicate
  effectively with deaf or hearing parents and siblings,
- the need for the child to be a full family member; that is to be a part
  of conversations and decisions within the larger family group as
  well as on an individual basis;
- the need for the child to have social contact with other deaf as well
  as hearing children outside of the school context;
- the need for the child to be able to understand and relate to the
  culture of the home, whether that be deaf or hearing culture,
  including minority language cultures;
- the need for the child to continue to learn about the world around
  him or her and to extend his or her general knowledge through
  explained experiences;
- the need for the child to develop independence within the home
  environment accompanied by a high level of self-regard and
  confidence; and
- the need for the child to experience some consistency between home
  and school in terms of information and expectations.

As a parent you may wonder how all of these needs can be fully addressed
for your child. We have therefore selected some case studies which
illustrate the very different ways in which families establish successful
communication at home.

Case Studies

The Johnson Family

Both parents are deaf. They have a 9 year old, severely deaf child, Mary and an older hearing child, Scott.

Language choices

Mother is confident and comfortable talking and signing at the same time (Sign Supported English, SSE) and she enjoys interaction with hearing friends and neighbours. She uses SSE primarily in the home and frequently uses finger-spelling for names and for English words where no single equivalent sign exists.

Father is more comfortable using British Sign Language (BSL) with all of the family unless other hearing adults or children are present. He only tends to use SSE with Mary when he is reading with her.

Scott is bilingual, in that he is a competent user of both BSL and English. He has largely adopted his mother's style of communication in the home, although in his communication with Mary and his father he is readily able to adapt his communication where needed by incorporating more BSL features.

Mary is already sensitive to the differences between BSL and SSE and has no problems understanding either. Her most confident mode of communication is BSL but she also uses SSE with clear lip patterns and some voice, although her speech is not always fully intelligible. She is able to adapt her own communication according to the situation which enables her to communicate confidently with deaf and hearing adults.

This particular family illustrate the importance of not making assumptions about deaf parents' use of BSL and their language preferences in the home setting. The choices these individuals have made clearly satisfy their communication needs as a family. Mary will be advantaged to some extent in the school setting because of her access to BSL in the home but careful attention will also have to be paid to her developing English skills, particularly her strategies for using spoken English.

The Clarke Family

Both parents are hearing. They have an 8 year old, profoundly deaf son, Daniel, and a 3 year old hearing daughter, Samantha.

Language choices

Both parents prefer to use SSE. They occasionally drop the signs altogether because Daniel lip reads well when he is familiar with the language context.

Both parents regularly attend BSL classes which they feel helps them with their use of SSE and to meet other parents with deaf children. They both have some reservations about using BSL with Daniel all of the time, as they concerned that it might limit his acquisition of English. Nevertheless, they do not hesitate to use BSL if communication problems arise with Daniel or where clarification is needed.

Daniel communicates with his parents by using spoken English and signs simultaneously. His speech is not fully intelligible but he uses very clear lip patterns and English word order. He is however, surpassing his parents in his acquisition of BSL, which he is rapidly learning through his contact with deaf adults and children in the school setting.

The Clarke family are clearly happier with English as the language of the home and it is not unusual for a hearing family with one deaf child to operate in this way. What is important here is the consistency the parents are providing in terms of their approach to communication and their commitment to making links with other similar families. Daniel is being exposed to a clear and supported model of English at home and the family have found a comfortable way of functioning effectively.

Daniel's language programme at school will continue to develop his English skills, particularly his use of signs in context, his spoken language skills and his writing skills to ensure that he is able to continue to communicate fluently at home and in the wider hearing world. In the school setting, Daniel's BSL skills will also be developed and monitored as it is possible that, for access to the full curriculum and continued academic development, BSL may become his preferred or dominant language. If however Daniel is making appropriate progress and is able to learn effectively through SSE then his language programme will reflect this.

The Ahmed Family

Both parents are hearing and Urdu is their first language. They have a 14 year old son, Issan, with a profound hearing loss and a 7 year old hearing son, Imraz, who has a severe hearing loss. Within the extended family, there are also two younger deaf cousins and a deaf uncle.

Language choices

The mother has only basic English skills but she regularly attends the BSL classes organised for the Asian mothers of deaf children in the city. Using the skills gained at this class, she has developed her own effective means of communication with her children, which involves the use of BSL signs along with 'home signs' which are culturally specific. She adds the use of some English into this when talking with the children, particularly about issues related to the school curriculum. She also uses some Urdu lip-patterns when discussing home and family-related issues.

Father is a more confident English speaker and although he is unable to attend the offered BSL classes, he too has developed his own style of communication with both Issan and Imraz. This involves the use of gesture and other visual support with some signs that he has learnt within the family setting.

Issan communicates with both parents and his brother using mainly sign language. His sign language at home incorporates the BSL signs he is learning at school as well as the 'home signs' that are more specific to the cultural context of his family situation.

This family are in a relatively linguistically complex situation in that they are using three languages (English, BSL and Urdu) in the home, as well as operating within three cultures. Little is known about Asian sign languages and there is therefore limited provision for families like this to learn what might be a more culturally appropriate sign language. Much can be done, however, to support them in other ways. This family have clearly been able to take advantage of some of the support available in terms of sign language tuition and have found their own ways of communicating successfully in the home.

The provision for Issan at school will necessarily involve opportunities for him to work with a deaf or hearing adult with the same cultural and linguistic background as himself so that he is able to learn about his own religion and culture and gain some insights into the spoken language of the home. School staff will have to work hard to ensure that this level of support for the family is maintained and that the communication links between home and school work well.

The Jenkins Family

Both parents are hearing. They have a 10-year-old daughter, Rebecca, who has a moderate hearing loss, and two other young children who have normal hearing.

Language choices

The primary language used by all the family is spoken English. Occasionally, some additional gestures or signs are used, particularly where communication is taking place in a noisy setting. On the whole, the family have adapted their lifestyle sufficiently to ensure that Rebecca is fully included in family interaction.

The mother attends a family support group with other mothers of deaf children, where she has learnt some basic sign language skills. She feels that this is useful because it has broadened her understanding of deafness and deaf culture and she feels more prepared should Rebecca's hearing loss deteriorate. Rebecca also has friends at school who use sign language and who regularly visit the home, and the mother feels that this mix of friends is very important for Rebecca's broader understanding of deafness and for her developing identity and self-esteem.

Rebecca prefers to use spoken English, both at home and at school, and her speech is fully understandable. Occasionally, when stuck for a word, Rebecca will draw on the sign skills she has acquired socially at school and these skills also enable her to mix with other deaf peers.

This family communicate comfortably in English providing that the conditions are right and they have adopted strategies for making this work. The level of Rebecca's hearing loss is a very significant factor in making this language choice a realistic and manageable one. The school will need to provide a carefully structured programme of support for Rebecca's continued development of spoken English and the mainstream learning environment will need to be scrutinised to ensure that she is working in appropriate listening conditions. It will also be to Rebecca's advantage if she has opportunities to continue to develop sign language skills for social purposes so that she retains her positive attitude towards, and understanding of other deaf children and adults.

As these case studies have illustrated, the child's level of hearing loss is just one of the factors along the continuum which has to be considered along with the make-up of the family (deaf or hearing parents and siblings), the language and the culture of the home, the preferred modes of communication of the parents and the children as well as the breadth of information and support provided for the whole family. Families have to make decisions which suit them and which present manageable options. The school system can then take this into account in their assessment of each individual's communication needs and put together a programme of support which builds on, and continues to develop these established language and communication skills.

Conclusion

Any child, born anywhere the world regardless of their racial, social or economic background, is capable of learning any language to which he or she is exposed. For most children, the successful development of at least one language is taken for granted. For deaf children, it is only through the combined efforts of parents and educators and a shared understanding of what each individual needs to achieve this that this language capability can be realised.

Ensuring that deaf children realise these universal goals requires open mindedness regarding approaches to communication and careful analysis of the information about each individual child. Communication issues in the education of deaf children are often polarised but as parents you will appreciate that these choices are not always as clear cut. This chapter has attempted to demonstrate a more positive and constructive approach by promoting the notion of a continuum of need along which all deaf children's communication needs can be successfully identified, described and addressed.

Summary

In this chapter we have discussed what is meant by communication and identified the central issues for deaf children and their families. Through individual case studies we have illustrated the range of communication abilities and language preferences that deaf individuals may present. Case studies of contrasting families have also been used to present a realistic overview of the sorts of communication choices families make in order to best meet the needs of their deaf children.

Additional Reading

Erting, C. (1994) *Deafness, Communication, Social Identity: Ethnography in a Preschool for Deaf Children*. Burtonsville, MD: Linstok Press.
    In Chapters 5–9 contrasting case studies of the language and communication choices of different deaf children and their families are described.

Part 3
Deaf Children and Sign Language

The goals of sign bilingualism are to enable deaf children to become bilingual and bicultural, and participate fully in both the hearing society and the 'Deaf World'. Deafness is not regarded as a barrier to linguistic development, educational achievement or social integration.

Pickersgill (1998: 89)

Chapter 6
Becoming Bilingual

In this chapter we will explore the language issues for deaf children. We will illustrate ways in which deaf children and adults use sign language and English and explain the concept of bilingualism. The term **sign bilingual** has become an accepted way of describing people who are bilingual in sign language and English. Whether or not your child currently uses sign language, a clearer understanding of sign bilingualism will support your understanding of the range of language issues for deaf children. The unique aspects of sign bilingualism, particularly those which have educational implications, will be introduced and examined in more depth in following chapters.

Throughout this book sign bilingualism is presented as a positive option for deaf children. Deaf children who are able to use both sign language and English in their everyday lives are likely to benefit in terms of their personal, social and educational development in several ways. These children will be able to mix with both deaf and hearing children and adults and make choices about friendship groups and social activities. These children are likely to feel secure about their own sense of self as their language abilities enable them to move between deaf and hearing groups and place themselves where they feel most comfortable. Sign bilingual deaf children are also likely to begin school with a secure or well developed primary language which will provide the essential foundation for their continued development and education.

Defining Bilingualism

We will begin by defining terms and establishing a clear idea of what is meant by bilingualism for deaf children. Individual bilingualism is concerned with the skills, attitudes, experiences and linguistic behaviour of people who use two or more languages in their everyday lives. It is these individual characteristics which will be our main focus of attention with regard to sign bilingual individuals. There are many facets to individual bilingualism to consider. To describe a bilingual person, we have to look not only at their language skills but also at the contextual and the cultural aspects of their bilingualism. A full description or profile of a deaf child's bilingualism enables parents and teachers to more effectively support their continued language development. In order to usefully describe a child's bilingualism we would need to ask the following questions.

Individual language skills

A bilingual person is rarely equally fluent in both language. They usually speak one language better than the other or use different languages for different purposes in different situations. A description which takes these factors into account will therefore certainly be more complex but more realistic. The questions about language include:

- What levels of skill does the individual have in speaking, reading and writing both languages?
- When, with whom and for what purpose does the individual use either language?

Individual cultural identity

All languages exist within, and are central to, a cultural context in that they are the vehicle for communicating the shared experiences, values and beliefs of a group. A bilingual person has to interact with both cultures and so may also be bicultural to some degree, although this will vary between individuals. The questions about culture include:

- How familiar is the individual with both cultures and to what extent does s/he identify with them?
- To what extent is the individual identified by the speakers of both languages as part of their culture?

Individual routes to bilingualism

An individual's experience of language learning, and external factors which influence this process, will shape their bilingualism and biculturalism. These significant details account for the differences between bilingual individuals and help us to understand how differing circumstances can affect the nature of an individual's bilingualism. The background and contextual questions include:

- In what circumstances has the individual learnt two languages?
- What are the environmental factors influencing the individuals continued development and maintenance of both languages?

With these questions in mind we can now consider how the terms 'bilingual' and 'bicultural' might apply to deaf children and adults.

Deafness and Bilingualism

If we define a bilingual person as someone who uses two or more languages in their everyday lives then deaf people who use sign language and a spoken or written language are also bilingual. It can be argued that most deaf people are bilingual although individual language preferences and areas of strength will vary. It is recognised that there are different paths to sign bilingualism and that individuals will have different language dominances. For example, there are those for whom sign language is a **preferred language** in that it is the most fully accessible and easily acquired language. By way of contrast, some individuals will have sufficient useful hearing to acquire spoken language as a preferred language but may also develop the necessary sign language skills to communicate in a social context.

The term 'preferred language' is used here to denote the language in which a bilingual deaf person finds it easiest to make an utterance in any area of experience at a given time. Preferred language does not only indicate a preference for, or a wish to use a particular language, rather the criterion of 'ease of use' is stressed which can be affected by many different social, psychological factors as well as the level of proficiency.

It is only recently that deaf people have begun to be considered in a positive way and accepted as bilingual and discussions and research in this area have begun to develop. Our understanding and knowledge in this field has developed because of significant research in the 1970s which established the following important facts about deafness and language development.

The integrity of natural sign languages

Natural sign languages are recognisable as unique languages in their own right with a distinct grammar and structure. They have the same underlying principles of construction as spoken languages. They are not simple gestural codes for the spoken language, in that each sign does not correspond to a word in spoken language. Although little is still known about the origins and history of different sign languages, our under-standing of the structure and the acquisition of sign languages has increased over the last 30 years.

Deaf children's sign language development

Deaf children who are sufficiently exposed to sign language, acquire and develop it as hearing children acquire a spoken language. Most deaf children of deaf parents pass through similar developmental sequences to hearing children, in terms of vocabulary growth followed by grammatical development. This parallel development begins at the pre-linguistic stage where deaf infants babble using their hands instead of their voices, thus engaging the parent in early communication. The emergence of deaf children's first signs coincides with the emergence of hearing children's first words and the respective growth of their vocabularies and mastery of grammatical structures also proceeds at a similar rate.

This important development in our understanding places deaf children who use sign language and a written/spoken language on a par with bilingual hearing children. This endorses the identification of deaf people as a linguistic minority instead of a disability group as discussed in Chapter 2. The rest of this chapter will consider what similarities the bilingual deaf child shares with the bilingual hearing child and then explore areas where deaf and hearing bilingualism diverge.

Deaf and Hearing Bilingual Language Proficiency

Language dominance

Deaf individuals who are bilingual in sign language and English are as diverse in their knowledge, use and experience of two languages as hearing bilinguals. In discussing their language competence, we need to move beyond the general descriptions of bilingual competence such as the following which, in reality, apply to very few individuals.

- complete mastery of two different languages (Oestreicher, 1974: 9)
- near-native control of two or more languages (Bloomfield, 1933: 56)

These early definitions can only be applied to a person who is equally fluent in both languages across a range of contexts. This is, however, a rare phenomenon as most people use their different languages for different purposes, depending on the audience and the situation.

The extent to which an individual might be described as bilingual is always relative, depending on each individual's skills. However, there are specific differences with regard to a deaf person's English skills which are unique to the context of sign bilingualism. Due to the effects of deafness, certain spoken language skills (such as speech production) may never be fully acquired by some deaf individuals. Deaf adults with a native command of sign language and skills in written English may choose not to use their voices because they are not able to hear themselves and monitor their own articulation, pitch or volume. Their equivalent spoken English skills may therefore include the use of English lip patterns without voice along with signs from BSL produced in English word order. Where 'spoken English' is referred to as part of the repertoire of a bilingual deaf person's skills, this is included in the range of strategies deaf people may use for face-to-face communication with hearing people who know little sign language.

The following classifications provide a useful means of broadly describing deaf people in terms of their bilingualism.

- *Sign language-dominant bilinguals*: Deaf people who feel more confident and comfortable expressing themselves in sign language and in understanding sign language with minimum skills in written and spoken English. English is a second or additional language.
- *Balanced bilinguals*: Deaf people who are confident and comfortable expressing themselves in both sign language and English and who are able to understand sign language and spoken and written English equally well.
- *English-dominant bilinguals*: Deaf people who are confident and comfortable expressing themselves in English and who are able to understand English (written, spoken or signed English) better than sign language. Sign language is a second or additional language. (Adapted from Kannapell, 1993: 17–18)

Within these groups, an individual's skills in written and spoken English will still vary considerably. So far there has been very little research which has attempted to measure the degree of bilingualism among deaf people and it is an area fraught with difficulties of methodology and definition. Using the dimensions of understanding of bilingualism in the general literature we can at least describe sign bilingual individuals more fully and develop our understanding of the potential range of proficiency in the different language areas.

Language mixing

Although sign language and English are two distinct languages, intermediate language varieties do exist, where there is overlap between the signed and the spoken language which serves a specific function. These varieties are often called contact signing or Pidgin Sign English.

They are usually the result of contact between deaf and hearing people where conscious language choices have to be made for communication to be successful.

Contact signing may be used by deaf people communicating with people who know some sign but who do not have native competence. This may be a hearing person or another deaf person with different language skills and experience. Contact signing may involve adding more English features to the sign language such as English lip-patterns, word order and perhaps some vocalisation. Contact signing is not a language in its own right but a mixing of the two languages. Although some features of both languages can be found in contact signing, both language systems are actually simplified or reduced and there are also some language structures found which belong to neither language. The relationship between the two languages of sign language and English and the contact varieties in the centre is often described in terms of a language continuum as illustrated in the following diagram.

The languages of deaf people ←——→ The languages of hearing people		
Sign languages	Contact sign (or Pidgin Sign English)	Spoken and written languages
←——→		
British Sign Language (BSL) American Sign Language (ASL) French Sign Language (LSF)		(Spoken) English (Spoken) French
		Manually coded spoken languages Spoken languages used with a manual code or cue to visually represent the features of the spoken language

Bilingual language use

A sign bilingual person may make use of their language repertoire differently, according to their communicative needs at a given time and depending on the situation. Language choices are sometimes made for very practical reasons. At other times there may be a more symbolic significance in the person's choice of language use because language is a powerful way of reflecting an individual's cultural and linguistic allegiances and identity. The following list provides some examples of the different factors which might influence language choice for a bilingual deaf or hearing person.

- *The individuals involved in the interaction.* It is important to consider each person's preferred languages; the relationship between them and their different attitudes, roles and status as all these will influence language choice.
- *The situation or the context of the interaction.* A formal setting such as work or education will lead to different type of language use to an informal setting such as social activities, entertainment or a family gathering.
- *What the interaction is about.* The topic of a conversation and the vocabulary or specific language being used will also significantly affect language choice.
- *The purpose or function of the interaction.* The practical purposes of the interaction will determine language choice (e.g. socialising, public speaking, greetings, etc.) as will the more symbolic functions such as expression of identity or affinity with a culture.

The following selection of examples illustrate how speakers, situation, topic and purpose might influence a sign bilingual person's language choices.

Participants/speakers	Likely language choice
Two deaf people who know each other socially for whom sign language is the preferred language	Sign language
A deaf person socialising with a mixed group of deaf and hearing people who have positive attitudes towards learning sign language	Sign language
A deaf person chatting in the pub with a mixed group of deaf and hearing people with varying sign language skills	Contact signing
A deaf employee talking to her/his hearing manager who is English and has an indifferent attitude towards sign language and very few skills	Spoken/written English
Two deaf adults in the local deaf club	Sign language
A deaf adult teaching in an educational context where sign language is valued and respected as a language with equal status to English	Sign language
A deaf adult in the bank or the shopping centre	Spoken/written English

Topic	Likely language choice
Talking about life experiences as a deaf person in a deaf family	Sign language
Teaching sign language	Sign language
Discussing a work or educational issue which involves new and specific English terminology	Contact signing
Purpose/function	
To include and be included by hearing friends in a social setting	Contact signing
Routine, daily greetings (shops, garage, neighbours)	Spoken English
To put across a political message about sign language and the linguistic rights of deaf people	Sign language

Cultural Issues

Defining culture

Culture concerns the shared experiences, values and beliefs of a group. Language can be identified as the most significant defining feature of a culture and also as the vehicle for the communication of that culture. This definition fully applies to deaf culture in that sign language is indeed the significant defining factor.

> Deaf culture is a powerful testimony to both the profound needs and the profound possibilities of human beings. Out of a striving for human language, generations of deaf signers have fashioned a sign language . . . . Out of a need to interpret, to make sense of their world they have created systems of meaning that explain how they understand their place in the world. That the culture of deaf people has endured . . . attests to the tenacity of the basic human needs for language and symbol. (Padden & Humphries, 1988: 121)

Deaf people who consider themselves as socially and culturally deaf and use sign language constitute a social group not unlike a minority spoken language group. This is why discussions about deaf culture bring us very much into a political arena. We are quite used to talking or reading about French culture, Asian culture, Jewish culture and we are immediately able to think of religious, geographical or linguistic characteristics of such groups. However, the notion of a 'deaf culture' is much more intangible and harder to quantify. Accepting the concept of a 'deaf culture' challenges our perspectives of deafness in that it requires us to think beyond deafness as a disability and to consider the broader social and linguistic implications.

> Unlike other cultures, deaf culture is not associated with a single place . . . rather, it is a culture based on relationships among people for whom a number of places and associations may provide common ground. (Lane *et al.*, 1996: 5)

As this quotation illustrates the notion of deaf culture does not relate to a particular place on a map but rather to what is often referred to as the 'deaf world' where people share the experience of what it is like to be deaf. The bonds, association and shared experiences that deaf people have developed with each other make up deaf culture. These bonds include, most importantly, a common language but also social and political organisations, artistic and literary expression as well as a shared experience of being a minority group within a majority society.

Some argue that it is the network of residential schools for the deaf that have enabled deaf culture to survive and to be passed down through generations. It is within these schools that many deaf people have acquired their sign language skills and, often lifelong, friendships. It is argued that this environment also enables young people to develop a strong sense of deaf identity and belief in themselves, thus equipping them to function effectively in deaf and hearing communities. The strong move towards the inclusion of deaf children into mainstream schools is therefore seen by some as a threat to sign language and deaf culture and to the individual's knowledge of deaf heritage and personal deaf identity.

When we start to reflect on deaf culture we also become aware that there must be such a thing as 'hearing culture' which we take for granted, but which deaf people are keenly aware of. It is only as we understand more about sign language and sign bilingualism that we can begin to unravel the complexities of the interaction between these two cultures. With this insight comes a recognition of the effort needed to ensure that these two cultures can achieve a positive co-existence based on mutual respect and understanding.

We have discussed the nature of a sign bilingualism and looked at parallels with hearing bilingualism. Similar comparisons can be drawn between deaf and hearing biculturalism. According to Grosjean's (1992) criteria, deaf people can be described as bicultural in that they live in two or more cultures and they adapt (at least in part) to these cultures and are able to blend aspects of these cultures. The following questions regarding cultural identity can therefore be applied to sign bilingualism.

Identification with a culture

Identification with a culture or a community is concerned with the extent to which an individual feels to be a part of that culture or community, is able to use the language in appropriate contexts and to participate comfortably in activities or events specific to that community. These notions have been explored in relation to deaf identity and culture and some descriptions of the variability in cultural identity in bilingual hearing people have been adapted to describe the parallel range with regard to sign bilingual individuals.

- Harmonious identification with both cultures (identifies with both deaf and hearing cultures and knows both languages);
- Identification with hearing culture and rejection of deaf culture (rejects BSL and deaf culture and identifies self as a hearing person, using English to communicate with hearing people);
- Identification with deaf culture and rejection of hearing culture (identifies with deaf people, uses BSL and participates in deaf social clubs and organisations); and
- Failure to identify with either culture (not able to identify with or comfortably participate in either culture and not skilled to a high level in either language). (Kannapell, 1993: 27)

Deaf individuals may find themselves at either extremes of this list or somewhere in the middle. They may be able to change their position although this is not always possible because, as well as personal choice, there may well be contextual factors which will affect the nature of deaf people's bilingualism and biculturalism such as their home background, their schooling or their contact with other deaf people. These contextual or background factors will be explored more fully later in this chapter.

Acceptance by a culture

Whether or not an individual is part of the deaf community and what constitutes a right to membership of that culture and community is a topic which has been hotly debated. It is an issue which concerns the place of hearing people within the deaf community and culture but it is also an issue between deaf people themselves with different backgrounds and language preferences.

A distinction is usually made between deaf people who see themselves as part of a cultural and linguistic group and deaf people do not strongly identify with deaf cultural values or the activities of the deaf community but rather see themselves a part of the hearing community. Often this distinction is indicated by using the description 'Deaf' with a capital 'D' to refer to the individuals who defines themselves as culturally deaf and the form deaf with a small 'd' for the individual who identifies more strongly with hearing culture. Although this is very much a simplified portrayal of the differences and divisions it serves to illustrate the possible sources of cultural conflict between deaf people themselves. A deaf individual may experience many dilemmas in trying to operate success-fully within both hearing deaf communities. Success in becoming an accepted member of the deaf community by other deaf people is not based on level or degree of hearing loss but on issues such as attitude to sign language; cultural values and beliefs; appropriate behaviour and social connections.

Membership of a community

Membership of the deaf community and identification with deaf culture is different for hearing people. Given the previously described prerequisites we can see how it could be argued that a hearing person can never fully be a part of the deaf community. A hearing person may only ever be able to be close to deaf culture, the most important prerequisites being an understanding and respect for deaf people and a fluent user of sign language. Oliver Sacks in his book (1989) argues that the only hearing people who are ever likely to be considered full members of deaf culture are hearing children of deaf parents for whom sign language is a natural language. There is a fine line however, between being accepted by a community and being identified as part of a culture. This is particularly true for those who are fluent sign language users such as partners and friends of deaf people, hearing people with deaf parents, interpreters and other hearing professionals who work regularly alongside deaf people.

Carol Padden (1991) who has written about deaf community and culture makes a distinction between being a member of the deaf community and being a member of the culture of deaf people. She suggests that community is more open in that it is a group of people who interact together on a regular basis and who share some of the same concerns and interests. Therefore a hearing person may well be identified as part of that community.

> A deaf community is a group of people who live in a particular location, share the common goals of its members, and in various ways, work towards achieving these goals. A deaf community may include persons who are not themselves Deaf, but who actively support the goals of the community and work with deaf people to achieve them. (Padden, 1991: 41)

Deaf and Hearing Bilingual Language Development

We have now explored the nature of sign bilingualism and biculturalism and looked into the main characteristics of a sign bilingual deaf
person's language, culture and identified and how these differ from
certain aspects of hearing bilingualism and biculturalism. Finally we will
consider the factors which affect the development and maintenance of a
bilingual person's two languages. In this section, we will focus our
attention much more on the deaf child and explore the interaction
between their development within the contexts of home, school and the
wider society.

Routes to bilingualism for hearing children

There are many routes to becoming bilingual which depend largely on
the individual's family circumstances, their educational experiences and
the wider social context. The different types of non-deaf bilingualism can
be split into three main groups.

Children from linguistic minorities

For these children, the home language or language of their parents is a
minority language. Usually the minority language does not have official
status so learning the majority language may be necessary for education
and future employment. These children become bilingual because they
learn the majority language through school and through their interactions
with the wider majority society. The success of this route to bilingualism,
in terms of the child's sense of personal identity and their academic
achievement, depends very much on the maintenance of the individual's
home language and on how appropriately their second language learning
(learning of the majority language) is managed in the school context.

Children from bilingual families

These children have parents with different first languages. These
children are likely to use and learn both languages at home depending
how the family has decided to use the two languages. Alternatively the
family may decide to use the foreign language exclusively at home in
which case the child will learn the official majority language through
school and other interactions outside the home. This route to bilingualism
has many advantages for the child who is likely to achieve a high level of
skill in both languages. The consequences of failing to become bilingual
through this route are unlikely to adversely affect either family relationships or educational success.

Children from linguistic majorities

These children learn another language in foreign or second language classes usually through school and sometimes out of choice. Their home language is the official majority language. There is unlikely to be any great pressure, either externally or from within the family, to become bilingual in contrast to the other two routes described and therefore the success of this route depends less on emotional and psychological factors and more on the effective teaching of the foreign language and individual ability. The consequences of failing to become bilingual through this route are unlikely to seriously affect either the child's sense of individual identity or their overall educational success and future employment prospects.

Routes to bilingualism for deaf children

Out of these three main routes the path to bilingualism for the deaf child is more like that of the child from the first group in that their preferred language is a minority language with no official status, educational or economic value within the majority culture. The closest parallel can be drawn between the hearing child whose home language is a UK minority language such as Punjabi or Hindi and the deaf child from a deaf family where sign language is the home language. Both the deaf and the hearing child are also in the situation of learning English in the school setting where the level of support for their home language will vary depending on educational policy.

There are, however, some significant differences which make the particular route a deaf child will follow both unique and, at times, difficult. Most linguistic minority children acquire their first language at home and from their immediate community and begin to acquire the second language at school. For the deaf child of deaf parents this is also likely to be the pattern and therefore a possible route to bilingualism will involve learning sign language naturally at home and English more formally in school setting.

For the deaf child of hearing parents, the experience may be different. Hearing families of deaf children are unlikely to have sign language skills when their deaf child is born and it may be that the family are learning sign language at the same time as the child is acquiring language. For a deaf child from a hearing family therefore the route to bilingualism may involve learning sign language and English at the same time. English will still be the language of the home and it is likely that a mixture of natural sign language, manually coded and spoken and written English will be used in that environment.

Other differences concern the learning of the majority language. For the deaf child from either a deaf or a hearing family there are other factors affecting developing language competence with the spoken form of the majority language. The deaf child is learning a second language which they cannot fully hear, whereas the hearing child has access to the second language which is not limited for any physiological reason. In addition to this, because sign language is a visual-gestural language there is no written form. This means that deaf children who are fluent sign language users will still not have had the experience of the written form of their language which some other hearing bilingual children do. When bilingual deaf children are learning to read and write they are also learning about an entirely new system of communication which requires very different skills to learning the conversational form of a language. Finally, many minority language bilingual hearing children live in communities where they are surrounded by other speakers of their language. They therefore see their language being used on a daily basis by other children and adults which confirms that they are part of a larger group of people like themselves. Deaf families who use sign language are not generally found to live in tight-knit communities such as this. A deaf child, particularly within a hearing family, is therefore more likely to feel isolated in their local community and will not benefit from the support and positive affirmation of their own culture and identity implicit in this infrastructure.

Factors Affecting a Child's Continued Bilingual Development

Given the right circumstances a bilingual child should continue to develop and maintain their first or home language and achieve a high level of second language competence. Whether or not this happens relies on a combination of contextual and individual factors. The child's very individual language learning skills and strategies will be significantly affected by the context in which they are developing both languages. For the child, the home and the school environments are likely to present the most significant developmental influences.

The home context

The home context is the child's starting point on the route to becoming bilingual and certain factors undoubtedly affect their progress along this route. The most important of these is successful communication between the child and the family. All children benefit from child-centred interaction and stimulating language experiences at home. For bilingual children, it is essential that their preferred language is well established prior to school entry. It may be that both languages are used at home or alternatively that the child's preferred language is established at home and the second language is introduced formally at school. Either of these situations will give the child the early language experiences they need providing the child and the family share positive and relaxed communication.

The educational context

The school setting is responsible not only for the effective education of bilingual children but it is also the place where society's values and attitudes are reflected through the policies in place and the language aims of the school. The role of schools in educating bilingual children therefore extends beyond the classroom in that the school experience is likely to reflect the challenges facing bilingual individuals both socially and in the world of work. Schools certainly can make a difference to successful bilingual education by prioritising the following issues both at whole school and policy level and within the classroom setting:

- incorporation of the child's home culture, language and values into the school curriculum,
- involvement of parents in their children's schooling,
- promotion of cultural diversity throughout the school,
- involvement of bilingual staff as language and role models,
- provision of language development and maintenance programmes for the child's preferred language,
- provision of appropriate second language instruction and
- appropriately high expectations of all bilingual students.

Individual factors

In a facilitative learning environment and with a secure home language background, a bilingual child is more likely to have a positive self-image and a confident sense of self-identity. This will greatly affect their continued development of both languages. The bilingual child is much more likely to be able to make the best of their language skills and enjoy the advantages of being bilingual when they are not under pressure to replace their preferred or home language with the dominant or majority language and where their preferred language is not devalued.

Separating an individual's language skills from the contextual factors which influence their development is very difficult. An individual's progress in the second language may be dependent on their level of skills in the first language or they may be adversely affected by the language learning situation. Some individuals, however, do learn languages and retain them more easily or quickly than others and this has implications for the teaching and learning situation and for the design of the second language learning programme. Different individuals may have different learning styles in that some may prefer to learn language very formally by learning rules and through repetition and drill whereas others may be better suited to a natural communicative approach which focuses on using language for real life purposes. Others may benefit from a balance of both approaches. It is important, therefore, that language learning programmes are flexible and well matched to the individual learning styles.

Conclusion

For sign bilingual children to continue to develop and maintain their English and sign language skills, both languages and cultures should be nourished and the child's bicultural identity should be recognised. This involves ensuring that the deaf child is given access to sign language at an early age and that they experience an appropriately sustained and monitored sign language development programme. The facilitating of good relationships with other deaf adults, both as language models and positive role models, is also a necessity.

The child's experiences with the second language must be meaningful and successful and they must be sufficiently motivated to persevere with learning a second language for this aspect of their bilingualism to continue to develop. This has very significant implications for educational policy and provision in terms of the place of sign language and the teaching of English both of which will be explored further in later chapters.

Summary

This chapter has provided an overview of the relationship between bilingualism and deafness and by doing so identified where spoken and sign bilingualism diverge. Although there are some parallels between sign and spoken bilingualism and biculturalism, there are some issues which are very specific to sign bilingualism particularly with regard to language development. To summarise we can see that the route to bilingualism for the deaf child is most like that of the hearing child from a linguistic minority and later in this book we will explore, in more detail, the educational implications of the similarities and the differences discussed.

Additional Reading

Baker, C. (1996) *Foundations of Bilingual Education and Bilingualism*. Clevedon: Multilingual Matters.

    The first section of this book provides an extensive overview of the individual and social nature of bilingualism in general.

Grosjean, F. (1992) The bilingual and the bicultural person in the hearing and in the deaf world. *Sign Language Studies* 77, 307–320.

    This paper explores the similarities and differences between deaf and hearing bilingualism.

Chapter 7

Deaf Children and Sign Language

Introduction

In this chapter we will consider deaf children who use sign language and English in their everyday lives. In the previous chapter we explained sign bilingualism and discussed the ways in which it relates to bilingualism in two spoken languages. As parents you will probably want to know more about the practical implications of sign bilingualism for your child's development. The goal of this chapter is therefore to move on from this broad perspective to look more carefully at these practicalities of meeting the social, emotional and educational needs of bilingual deaf children both at home and at school. You may not consider your individual child to be sign bilingual or to be developing both languages, however, the issues discussed in this chapter should help to answer some of your questions about different deaf children's routes to language development.

The foundation provided by the initial chapters has demonstrated the importance of placing sign bilingualism within a broad and balanced framework which recognises the diversity of individual needs and experiences. A linguistic and cultural model of deafness is central to this chapter in that, while the medical implications of deafness are acknowledged, the linguistic needs of the deaf child are considered to be paramount and we present bilingualism as a positive factor in the child's overall development.

An Introduction to Sign Language

Any discussion about the development and education of deaf children is incomplete without reference to sign language. You may have found that getting full information in this area has been difficult; it is therefore our intention to redress this balance. Throughout this book, sign language is central to discussions of deafness both in terms of the developing child and in consideration of educational provision. We stress that deaf children's communication needs should be seen on a continuum along which language dominance's will vary. Sign language is not considered as a remedial option, or last resort, for individual children who are not succeeding to develop spoken language to the level of their hearing peers.

However small or large a part sign language may play in your child's education, it is still useful for you to have an insight into the properties and development of sign language as compared to spoken languages. This section of the chapter will provide you with some of that background information by giving an overview of current understanding of sign language and of its development in young deaf children.

The discovery of sign language

It is only relatively recently that sign languages have been discovered and accepted as 'real languages'. The most well known pioneering research into the properties of sign languages was carried out by William Stokoe in 1960 at Gallaudet University in the United States. This, and other early research into sign languages, concentrated largely on the linguistic description of sign language. This means that emphasis was placed on the identification of its distinctive features and of a grammar system. The main outcome of this early research was the discovery that sign languages share the same fundamental properties as spoken languages such as:

- they are governed by a rule system,
- they exhibit dialects according to geographical factors,
- they change over time to accommodate changes in society (technology, etc.) and
- they can be acquired by young children without systematic instruction as a preferred system of communication.

Research into sign languages convinced linguists that they possess the same characteristics as all other natural human languages and this led to a review of the concept a 'natural human language'. The recognition of sign languages as fully-fledged human languages requires us to accept that language can be perceived and conveyed through more than one modality, that is through vision and gesture as well as through hearing and speech.

The linguistics of sign language

Sign language is not an international language. Deaf people from different countries use different sign languages. The hundreds of sign languages that are used all over the world are as distinct from each other as spoken languages are and all have the same richness and potential. Thus American Sign Language (ASL) is the equal of British Sign Language (BSL) as are sign languages in Japan, Russia or even Iceland (where there are less than 100 deaf people). There is evidence that sign language has been used since the 1600s in Britain although the term 'British Sign Language' was first used by Mary Brennan as recently as 1976. This official recognition of BSL as a bona fida language marked the beginning of more intense and focused research into BSL, its properties and developmental features. The way in which sign language is expressed cannot easily be conveyed through pictures or diagrams. We have therefore recommended some video sources of introductory material at the end of this chapter.

One way of describing a language is as a system of small building blocks or units. For spoken languages we understand that these building blocks are:

- the sounds (phonology),
- the vocabulary (lexicon),
- the grammar (syntax).

The individual sounds within a particular spoken language are not meaningful by themselves until they are combined with other sounds to form words. The grammatical component can be subdivided into the smallest units of language which convey grammatical information (morphology), such as verb endings, and the grammar that holds larger sequences of language together, such as sentences (syntax).

BSL can also be analysed into these component parts although they are expressed through a visual rather than an oral mode. Sign languages are made up of individual signs which are organised to create a coherent grammatical system. In sign languages the smallest building blocks are also known as phonological units. These are the components of manual signs such as the shape of the hand, where the hand is and the direction in which it is moving. The grammar of sign language also exploits the visual properties of the language in that is expressed through the place of signs and the relationship expressed between signs. It is these unique features that have drawn attention to the study of sign language within the wider field of linguistic research.

Children's development of sign language

Despite the fact that sign languages differ from spoken languages in a number of significant ways, it has been established that the progression through the stages of development for both languages is very similar. The stages of language development which have been explored include:

- pre-linguistic communication (7–10 months),
- the first-sign/word stage (12–18 months),

- the two-sign/word stage (18–22 months),
- the more complex lexical and grammatical development (22–36 months).

The studies of BSL development have usually been with deaf children of deaf parents who have had access to BSL from birth and this has enabled researchers to consider BSL development in parallel with spoken language development.

One of the first significant similarities which has been identified concerns the role of babbling in pre-linguistic development. Vocal babbling enables hearing children to tune into and rehearse the sounds of the language they are developing and to engage in early interaction with their carers. It has been found that deaf children who are exposed to sign language also babble but manually, in that they move their hands and arms in a specific repetitive way thus engaging the carer in communicating.

At the one sign/word stage, deaf children produce individual signs in isolation, these usually include the sign POINT and as well as basic nouns and verbs such as MUMMY and DRINK. Deaf children develop their vocabularies at the same rate as hearing children acquire spoken vocabulary often overgeneralising, e.g. using DOG for all four-legged animals or making errors in their sign productions in the same way that hearing children grapple with the articulation of new words. Some researchers have argued that the rate of acquisition of signs may be faster than that of words. This may be because the control of the vocal apparatus is harder to master than control of the hands or that the iconicity (visual similarity with the object) of some signs makes them easier to acquire. However, these differences tend to even themselves out and the general markers for hearing children of 10 words at 15 months and 50 words at 20 months also to apply to deaf children's sign vocabulary development.

The similarity of rate and nature of the development of two languages is also evident at the two-word stage. In both signed and spoken language the two-word stage emerges at about the same time and the typical utterances are isolated single words without grammatical markings such as TEDDY COT or MUMMY WORK.

As deaf children begin to extend their sign language utterances between the age of 2 and 3 years they begin to use a wider range of the grammatical conventions of sign language. One indication of the child's developing sophistication with sign language grammar is their use of verb agreement. With regard to sign language this refers to the way in which a verb moves from its subject to its object location. Where this convention is used I–GIVE–YOU can be expressed through a one-sign utterance rather than the use of a sequence of three signs which is what a younger deaf child might do. At around the age of 3 years, deaf children are also able to change the standard use of a verb to give additional adverbial information such as how an action is carried out.

Although there is very little research into the development of deaf children's sign language between the ages of 3 and 6 years, the evidence collected so far indicates that the rate of grammatical development parallels that of spoken languages. As with spoken language, it is argued that exists a critical period of development beyond which it becomes difficult to gain a complete mastery of grammar. This is thought to be around the age of 5 years for both spoken and signed languages. It is interesting to note, however, that deaf children who have not been exposed to sign language before the age of two can still acquire the same levels of fluency as those exposed to sign language from birth.

These findings regarding sign language underline the biological capacity that young children possess for developing language whatever its modality. Children are only exposed to a fraction of all of the possible grammatical structures in their language and yet they are able to construct their own representation of the language from this input. This is called nativisation. The nativisation theory holds that children use their native or innate ability to construct the grammar of a language from only limited input. This theory explains, in part, why deaf children who are only ever exposed to a manual form of English, rather than natural sign language (BSL or ASL), still create language patterns which occur in natural sign language.

The information that has been collected over the last 30 years about patterns of BSL acquisition has provided the basis for the development of an assessment tool for BSL. This is a much needed development as it will allow deaf children's progress in sign language to be measured for the first time. The increasing interest in sign bilingual education programmes for deaf children points to a need for a standardised measure of sign language assessment as a way of monitoring the outcomes of such programmes. The assessment focuses on receptive and productive BSL grammar and will provide norms for children age 3–11 years. This is a landmark development for parents and all professionals involved with deaf children as it is a firm endorsement of the changing status of BSL and of the goals of sign bilingual education.

Other Signing Systems

You will be aware that there are several other ways of communicating using signs or manual gestures which cannot be described as natural sign languages such as ASL or BSL. This is a complex but important area for parents as few are fluent in sign language and many rely on other types of signing systems. Several sign systems have been developed with the aim of making English visually accessible to deaf children. These sign systems are distinct from BSL or ASL as naturally evolving languages although many of them use signs from BSL and ASL in English word order to parallel the spoken message. You are likely to find that some terms used to describe deaf children's communication such as 'manual communication' or 'signing' are vague and need explanation. Where you can, it is important to try to find out whether a natural sign language, such as BSL, or an English-based signing system is being referred to. In addition to these consciously developed systems, language mixing between BSL and English also occurs naturally as a result of sustained contact between deaf and hearing individuals and communities.

The following list of definitions of some of the terms used to describe these different signing systems are adapted from Lane *et al.* (1996).

Sign System	Abbrev.	Description
British Sign Language American Sign Language	BSL ASL	Complete and naturally evolving languages which differ in lexicon and syntax from English and from each other
Pidgin Sign English Contact sign	PSE	The contact varieties of sign language which include elements of both BSL and English and which are a result of the interaction between deaf and hearing people
Sign Supported English Simultaneous Communication	SSE sim-com	A visual/gestural representation of some parts of English (usually content words) where speech and signs are produced at the same time
Manually Coded English	MCE	An umbrella term for the number of different sign systems which aim to fully represent English through the use of signs borrowed from BSL and the use of made-up signs to represent some of the grammatical information which have no equivalent in BSL, such as articles, prefixes, suffixes and word endings

Sign System	Abbrev.	Description
Signed English Seeing Exact English	SE SEE	Two of the MCE systems most commonly referred to in Britain and the USA
Cued Speech	CS	A system of handshapes used in certain locations around the face alongside spoken language to visually convey all of the 40 phonemes (sounds) of English
Paget-Gorman		A contrived sign system used for representing the vocabulary and grammar of spoken English where the signs are not drawn from BSL
Makaton		A contrived specifically selected sign system used for basic communication with deaf and hearing children with complex needs
Finger-spelling		The use of the manual alphabet to represent each letter of English (this is two-handed in Britain and one-handed in the USA) NB: Finger-spelling also occurs naturally within BSL, for example for initialisation and naming

Describing Sign Bilingual Deaf Children

The broad definition we have used to describe bilingual deaf children encompasses all those who use sign language and written and/or spoken English in their everyday lives. This definition brings together a diverse range of children who cannot be considered as a homogenous group in terms of their linguistic needs and experiences. As we established in the previous chapter, the individual nature of a child's bilingualism should be recognised and can be better understood if the following questions are addressed.

The individual child's path to bilingualism

- In what circumstances has the deaf child learnt sign language and English?
- How is the child being enabled to develop and maintain both languages?

The individual child's language use and preferences

- What levels of skill does the deaf child have in their receptive and expressive use of both sign language and English?
- When, with whom and for what purposes does the deaf child use either language?

The individual child's cultural identify and self-image

- How familiar is the deaf child with both deaf and hearing cultures and to what extent does they identify with them?
- To what extent is the deaf child identified by other deaf and hearing peers and adults as part of their culture?

We shall now explore each of these areas focusing specifically on deaf children. This will demonstrate the diversity within this group of children in terms of their bilingualism and provide a basis for more in-depth discussion of developmental and educational issues.

Paths to Bilingualism

For your child it may be that becoming bilingual is essential not optional as they cannot access their entire education through spoken and written English. This is the case for many deaf children. For these children it is far more likely that they will be able to achieve mastery of a sign language, rather than of a spoken language. It is also important to acknowledge that being deaf and bilingual does not have to mean that sign language is the preferred or primary language. It could be that spoken language emerges as your child's first language, and sign language is acquired later in specific circumstances for specific purposes. There is more than one path to becoming bilingual and using the home and the family as the starting point we will look at the three main routes.

Early access to sign language

For a small minority of deaf children the path to bilingualism is relatively straightforward in that they grow up with an opportunity to acquire sign language naturally as a preferred language: 10% of all deaf children have at least one deaf parent and are likely to be exposed to some sign language within the home environment. It is also possible that deaf families will have a network of family and friends experienced in deafness and sign language. Research has shown that these children are able to acquire fluency in sign language at the same rate as hearing children acquire a spoken language and that they also go through parallel stages in their language development. The path to bilingualism for these children could be described as sequential bilingual development in that they are not likely to be exposed to spoken English until school age. By this time they will have a sufficiently well developed first language to enable them to participate in an age-appropriate curriculum.

Later access to sign language

For deaf children of hearing parents, which is the majority of deaf children (over 90%), the path to bilingualism may not be so smooth. These children are born into families which take hearing and speaking for granted and which are not necessarily structured according to the needs of a deaf child. Deaf babies in this situation begin life without the same level of contact through sound that hearing babies enjoy with their parents and without the tactile and visual experiences that a deaf parent would intuitively know how to provide. Hearing parents also have significant emotional and practical adjustments to make during this crucial time as they may know very little about deafness and about how to modify their communication, their environment and their expectations. Most parents will quickly adopt a visual form of communication with their deaf child and some will learn a variety of sign language. This group of deaf children may still miss out on the early experience of exposure to the richness and complexities of adult language which is specifically directed towards them as young language learners.

The degree to which different hearing parents are able to provide a sign language environment at home will vary tremendously and some parents will be more confident communicators in sign language than others. What this group of children do share, however, is that without exception they will have experienced two different ways of communicating from a very early age in that they will have been simultaneously exposed to a spoken and a signed language. Most of these children will arrive at school with emerging skills in both languages and a readiness to be immersed in a sign language environment at which point their bilingual language skills can begin to be nurtured and channelled.

Describing deaf children in this way illustrates that a deaf child with one or more deaf parents is more likely to achieve an age-appropriate level of proficiency in sign language prior to school entry than a deaf child of hearing parents. This assumes that deaf parents choose to use sign language as their preferred language and as the language of the home. Some deaf parents may prefer to use English with their deaf child. So although these two different paths to bilingualism offer potentially different opportunities, there can no guarantee that either child will arrive at school with age-appropriate sign language skills. For all of these children, priority must be given to the continued development of sign language as a primary language and to the development of spoken and/or written English as a second or additional language.

Sign bilingual partially hearing children

In contrast to the two groups described previously, the path to bilingualism may well involve an element of choice for some deaf children who have sufficient levels of hearing to successfully acquire spoken English as a preferred language. These children may, however, become bilingual because it becomes evident at some point in their schooling that they will benefit from learning and mixing socially in a sign language environment. For this group of children, sign language may never become a preferred language, but may play a crucial role in their development both educationally and socially. It may be the social needs of the child which motivate the parents to ensure that they meet deaf peers and adults who use sign language. Alternatively, the parents and teachers involved with the child may feel that access to sign language in the learning context would provide him or her with the additional linguistic support needed to achieve academically. Whatever the motivation behind this decision, the children in this group will also develop bilingual skills in English and sign language but probably to a different degree and via a different route from those in either of the other two groups.

To expose partially hearing children, whose preferred language is English, to sign language is not considered to be detrimental to the development of their spoken language skills. Their bilingualism will be an asset to them, not a disadvantage, as they are likely to experience benefits in terms of their cognitive, linguistic and social development. In Sweden, where bilingual educational programmes for deaf children are well established, a growing number of parents want their partially hearing children to attend the schools for deaf so that they can enjoy the social and educational benefits of being in a sign language learning environment. For these bilingual deaf children then, priority should be given to their continuing development of age-appropriate spoken and written English skills and to the development of sign language as a second or additional language.

Bilingual Education

While the home context is a key factor in identifying different individual paths to bilingualism, the school setting also plays a crucial part in ensuring that individual linguistic needs are recognised and that both languages are successfully developed and maintained. The different paths to bilingualism we have explored illustrate how and why deaf children might arrive in school with varying levels of skill in sign language and English. The educational model which is going to be the most appropriate for these children will be one which recognises this and which is able to respond to the diversity of language needs these individuals present.

The ideal educational approach for all deaf children should be one which provides them with equal opportunities to achieve academic and vocational success on a par with their hearing peers. For deaf children who are bilingual in sign language and English an approach which recognises the equal status of these the languages can most effectively meet this educational entitlement. The fundamental principle of a sign bilingual approach is that all children have the opportunity to attain age-appropriate skills in their preferred language thus providing the linguistic foundation necessary to tackle the demands of the curriculum as well as the learning of an additional or second language.

> [This approach] will seek to nourish both the languages and culture of the Deaf community and the languages and cultures of the hearing community. Linguistic and cultural incorporation affirms the deaf child's identity as a Deaf, sign language using child, whilst at the same time, recognising the child's identity as part of (at least) one other community within the wider hearing society. (Brennan & Brien, 1995: 259)

You may have found that the goals of a bilingual approach are often misrepresented as focusing solely on sign language development or on deaf cultural issues. This can be misleading and confusing for parents. You may be concerned, that if your child learns to sign, it will isolate them from mainstream society and that this approach will preclude them from learning English. It is therefore extremely important that parents are fully aware of what a bilingual approach can offer their child. The central goals outlined below illustrate both the balance and the breadth offered within a sign bilingual approach and the emphasis placed on valuing individual differences among deaf children and their families.

Goals of a sign bilingual approach
- to ensure the successful acquisition of an age-appropriate preferred language as a basis for learning a second language;
- to provide access to the wider curriculum in the child's preferred language and opportunities for age-appropriate academic achievement;
- to facilitate the development of a positive self-image and cultural identity providing opportunities for full participation in both the deaf community and the wider hearing society.

It is difficult to envisage how such far-reaching goals might be practically attained. Indeed these goals do require the establishment of sound educational policies as well a commitment to the consistent implementation and evaluation of such policies in practice. Sign bilingual approaches which are committed to practically achieving these goals should share the following characteristics:

- Deaf adults are directly involved in the children's education both at policy level and within the teaching and learning context.
- Hearing adults are themselves bilingual and have a positive attitude to the use of sign language with deaf children.
- Sign language and spoken/written languages are treated as separate but equal languages.
- Manually Coded English systems are recognised as tools for supporting the development of spoken and written English skills but not as the sole teaching medium.
- Individual language programmes for spoken/written language and sign language provide a structured plan for addressing each child's linguistic and communicative needs.
- Sign language (BSL, ASL etc.) is taught as a curriculum subject and individual progress is monitored and assessed.
- English is taught and assessed as a second language where written English is recognised as more accessible than spoken English.
- Each individual's aural and oral potential is maximised through appropriate audiological management and speech training programmes.
- The children have access to the same breadth of curriculum and the same assessments as their hearing peers through their preferred language.
- All communities and cultures within the school are equally valued and actively involved.
- Families are provided with the opportunity to become actively involved in their children's education and to learn sign language themselves within the school context.

Many schools and services for deaf children include the use of sign language or Manually Coded English systems in their approach to the education of deaf children but this does not necessarily mean that they offer genuine bilingual provision. The crucial factor which distinguishes bilingual from other more eclectic approaches (sometimes known as Total Communication approaches) is the overall educational goal. A school or service may incorporate sign language or Manually Coded English into their teaching but the overall educational goal for all the children may still be essentially a monolingual goal of proficiency in spoken and written English. In contrast, established bilingual programmes such as those found in the UK, Scandinavia and North America, work proactively towards developing the children's bilingual skills in a spoken/written language and the sign language of the deaf community and in the children's home language if this is different from the majority language.

Language Use and Preferences

We have seen that each deaf child's route to bilingualism is very individual, depending initially on what choices are made in the home setting and, later on, what opportunities are provided in the school setting. The nature and extent of each child's skills in either language will also be unique depending how they use each language in different situations. Bilinguals are rarely equally fluent in both of their languages and usually gravitate towards a preferred or dominant language. Most bilingual people function differently in their two languages in different aspects of their lives and so have strengths and weaknesses in different areas. The groups of deaf children we will now describe illustrate how this individuality in terms of language use, skills and preferences relates to bilingual deaf children. To describe these children's varying bilingual skills, we have focused on how they use their languages for learning and on how they use their languages in a social context.

English-dominant sign bilingualism

For this group of children, spoken English is the first and preferred language. English is the language through which they are able to learn most efficiently and the language through which they will access most of the curriculum. English is the language in which they will develop their most sophisticated language skills including literacy skills which will develop later than speaking and listening skills. The reason for calling these children bilingual is because they also have receptive and expressive skills in sign language. Although they are learning spoken English on a par with their hearing peers, they also benefit from learning in a sign language environment and from interaction with deaf peers. They are better able to succeed in English because of the additional visual support for their curriculum learning and the extra support with oracy and literacy development which a bilingual environment will offer, such as specifically differentiated activities and small group work. Learning in a bilingual environment will also provide them with the opportunity to socialise with deaf peers and adults in sign language. This can provide welcome respite from concentrating solely on the spoken form which is very demanding even with a mild hearing loss. The balance of language skills typical of this group can be summarised as follows:

- spoken and written language skills to a level of proficiency sufficient to provide a basis for continued intellectual development;
- receptive sign language skills to a level of competence sufficient to benefit from additional support provided for curriculum access and the development of literacy skills; and
- expressive sign language skills to a level of competence sufficient for socialising and engaging in day to day interaction/conversation with deaf peers and adults.

Sign-language-dominant sign bilingualism

For this group of children, sign language is the preferred and dominant language. Sign language is the language through which they are able to learn most efficiently and the language through which they will access most of the curriculum. Sign language is the language in which they will develop their most sophisticated language skills and which will provide them with the intellectual and cognitive skills they need to learn English as a second or additional language. In terms of spoken English, these children's skills will be very variable ranging from those who are able to acquire some speech skills naturally, to those who will have a very limited potential for developing intelligible speech. The oral/aural skills of these children may fulfil a social and functional role such as day-to day conversation but will not be sufficiently developed to enable them to succeed academically in a speech-only educational environment. The development of these children's literacy skills will therefore be facilitated by any speaking and listening skills that the children have but will also rely on formal instruction through sign language. The balance of language skills typical of this group can be summarised as follows:

- sign language skills to a level of proficiency sufficient to provide a basis for continued intellectual and cognitive development;
- literacy skills to a level of proficiency depending on the individual's progress and experience as an English second language learner;
- receptive (listening and watching) English skills to a level of proficiency depending on the learner's use of residual hearing, lip-reading skills, and ability to use contextual and visual cues; and

- expressive spoken English skills to a level of competence depending on the individual's use of voice, intelligible speech and/or lip patterns.

Developing sign bilingualism

The children described in previous groups are at opposite ends of a continuum of need in terms of their level of language skills in sign language or English. What the children in both of these first two groups share, however, is a clearly defined dominant or preferred language in which they should have near age-appropriate skills. This third group of children differs, as we cannot say that they arrive at school with an age-appropriate preferred or primary language although they may have developing skills in both sign language and English. This group of children is, in fact, representative of the large majority of bilingual deaf children and if we look back to the different paths to bilingualism, we can see that they are most likely to be the deaf children of hearing parents. These children are in a complex linguistic situation because they may not come into contact with sign language (which will ultimately be their preferred language) until they arrive in school, even though at home some signing or gesture might be used with spoken English. The school setting might be their first experience of sustained exposure to sign language as used by deaf adults and by other deaf peers.

The balance of these children's skills can usually be identified to some extent as they begin to gravitate towards either sign language or English as a preferred language. However the route they will follow cannot be assumed without careful monitoring and assessment of their relative strengths and preferences in sign language and English. Language programmes can then be designed which provide an appropriate balance of language exposure and formal teaching in the relevant language. Educators also have to be aware that language preferences may change as a child moves up through school. This can be as a result of a change in the nature of the child's hearing loss, the increased complexity and demands of the language of the curriculum or linked to motivational, social or emotional reasons. The common need shared by all the children in this group is, therefore, for a preferred language to be successfully established. Until this is so, we cannot describe a specific pattern of language uses and preferences although we can identify some characteristics typical of this group:

- They are likely to arrive at school with developing sign language skills to a level of proficiency sufficient to engage in day-to-day interaction/conversation with deaf peers and adults.

- They are likely to arrive at school with emerging spoken language skills sufficient to engage in day-to-day interaction/conversation with hearing peers and adults.
- They may demonstrate more complex skills or some preference for one language but neither language will be developed to an age-appropriate level.
- They may frequently switch between languages depending on the level of complexity of what they are trying to communicate and the skills available to them in either language.
- In their own communication they may rely heavily on the use of signs with voice and are not yet fully aware of the separate nature of English and sign language.

Deaf children from minority ethnic groups

Children whose home language is a spoken language but not the majority language will also fall into one of these three groups. Some of these children will develop age-appropriate spoken language skills in the majority language and language of the home, although the domain of use of the two languages will be very different. These children may also benefit from learning and socialising within a bilingual setting. A few of these children will have siblings or parents who use sign language at home and so will arrive in school with near age-appropriate sign language skills and ready to learn English as their second or third language. The majority of these children, however, will arrive at school with some developing skills in sign language (which may include some 'home signs') and in a spoken language. To meet the educational and social-emotional needs of these children, additional provision must be made for them which respects, promotes and makes available to them the language and heritage of their home culture.

Cultural Identity and Self-image

In our consideration of sign bilingual deaf children so far, we have focused on the key language issues of routes to bilingualism and patterns of language use. Bilingualism necessarily exists alongside biculturalism and so the bilingual deaf child's social and cultural identity is an essential factor which must be considered. The term 'deaf culture' is often used quite vaguely to explain differences between deaf and hearing people or to refer to events at the deaf club or features of local deaf organisations. For some hearing parents the term 'deaf culture' may evoke concerns about an unknown but powerful entity. The culture of deaf people has many similarities to other language minority cultures which exist within a majority culture. The essential features of this community in Britain include:

- a thriving and active deaf community of approximately 50,000 people,
- a language which is used by approximately 1 in 1000 of the population as their only or preferred language,
- traditions (knowledge and experiences shared by deaf people across generations) and
- art forms (performance and visual arts including theatre, poetry, dance).

Bilingual deaf children may identify with this culture to a lesser or greater degree depending on the individual. The educational system must support this by valuing and making available to the children the language and culture of the adult deaf community. A study into sign bilingual deaf children's emerging sense of self and language awareness revealed that the deaf children within sign bilingual programmes were able to talked positively about their deafness and about the differences between deaf and hearing people. The children demonstrated an understanding of the differences between sign language and English and were able to discuss the importance of both languages for their future lives. Their educational experiences had equipped them with a basic understanding of their own deafness, deaf culture and deaf identity. They are secure in their understanding of their own deafness and their vision of their future as deaf adults (Gregory, Smith & Wells, 1997).

How deaf children see themselves and how they understand the concepts of deaf and hearing is likely to affect their sense of identity and self-esteem which may, in turn, influence their academic success. It is important that biculturalism is not seen as an ability to exist as a deaf and a hearing person in two separate realities but, as Padden (1994) describes, as an ability to recognise and negotiate differences and tensions between deaf and hearing people. Ladd (1991) describes his own realisation of this and how it enabled him to see himself and his relationship with hearing people more positively:

> Now I realised that I was really was an extrovert who had been repressed by having a false identity forced on me which offered me no support. That doesn't mean you stop talking with hearing people. On the contrary, the confidence you have gained gives you *more* chance to meet and mix with hearing people, because once you accept who you are you can accept the fact that you cannot hope to get all that is said and you adjust your behaviour accordingly. (Ladd, 1994: 96)

Schools can make a significant impact in this area by providing the context for the meeting of the deaf and hearing cultures where both are respected and promoted. Children are thus given opportunities to learn about differences between the two cultures as well as opportunities to interact with both cultures which will equip them with the knowledge, experiences and confidence they need to shape their own cultural and social identity.

Conclusion

We have demonstrated in this chapter how sign bilingualism might be practically applicable to your deaf child. You will realise that there is no one set route to bilingualism for all deaf children and that sign language will fulfil different linguistic needs for each individual child. You may recognise your child as belonging to the sign-language-dominant or the spoken-language-dominant group of children described. Alternatively you may not yet be sure which route they may take. Whatever your situation this information should support and inform your observations and decisions.

If sign language is to play a significant part in your child's development you will want to ensure that their needs are fully met in the educational context. This chapter will have given you an idea of what you are looking for in this respect. We have underlined the breadth of expertise that educators need in order to be able to offer appropriate educational provision. This expertise must include a specialised knowledge and understanding of the special nature of sign bilingualism and implications for the development of the deaf child's sign language and English skills, curriculum knowledge and social identity. Deaf and hearing professionals working with these children need to be prepared to address the range of linguistic needs that children present when they arrive at school, whatever their language experiences and dominances. This should be an entitlement for all deaf children and it is your right, as a parent, to expect this level of support for your child.

Summary

In this chapter we have concentrated on deaf children who use sign language to some extent in their everyday lives. In order to clarify terminology used in this area we have provided a description of sign language and of the different sign systems developed to support spoken language. We have described different routes by which deaf children might become sign bilingual using the family and the home setting as the starting point. We have established that it is rare to find bilingual individuals with an equal balance of skills in both of their languages and illustrated how language dominances will vary from child to child. We have presented the sign bilingual educational approach as one which can meet the needs of bilingual deaf children whatever their individual language preferences. What you would expect a sign bilingual approach to provide has also been identified. Finally, the social and emotional needs associated with cultural identity have been explored and exemplified through personal experiences.

Additional Reading

Woll, B. (1998). Development of signed and spoken languages In S. Gregory, P. Knight, W. McCracken, S. Powers and L. Watson (eds) *Issues in Deaf Education* (Chapter 2.2). London: Fulton Press.
  This chapter outlines the similar development process and properties of signed and spoken languages and describes the early stages of sign language development

Gregory, S., Smith, S. and Wells, A. (1997) Language and identity in sign bilingual deaf children. *Deafness and Education (BATOD)* 21(3), 31–8.
  This article reports on research into deaf children's identity in sign bilingual settings.

Video Material

Miles D. (1988) *British Sign Language: A Beginners Guide.*
  This is useful for anyone interested in sign language, particularly parents of deaf children and those with deaf friends, neighbours, relatives or colleagues.

Mason C. (1994) *The British Sign Language Video Phrase Book* (tapes 1 and 2).
  Two popular one-hour videos for beginners showing commonly used BSL phrases in such topic areas as greeting, family, time, number, health, school, work, travel and holidays.

L. Allsop and C. Mason (1987) *British Sign Language: A Beginner's Guide* (1987).
  An excellent video resource for learning BSL and for learning about deaf culture.

Part 4
Going to School

It is important to acknowledge not only how deaf children are like other children, but the very important ways they differ from other children. How does perceiving one's world visually make a difference in approaching various tasks?

Mahshie (1995: 57)

Chapter 8
Educational Choices

Introduction

Where deaf children will go to school is an issue of central and immediate concern to all parents and the professionals involved with them. Early on parents are faced with choices about the most appropriate educational setting for their child. It is important to remember that the educational needs of deaf children are no different from any other child going to school. It is the same for all children; that is to have access to a school setting which will give them the fullest opportunity to reach their potential, socially, personally and academically. This is largely accomplished through appropriate social interactions and successful academic experiences.

Before any decisions about placement can be made, parents need to understand, first, that there is a range of personal and educational issues to be considered and, second that choice of educational placement will be closely linked to the style of communication each child prefers (see Chapter 5). The issues of language and communication style are an essential part of any discussion about the choice of educational placement.

It is acknowledged that the whole area of method of communication and educational choices in the education of deaf children has long been a matter of controversy and debate. It is interesting to place that debate in its historical context. This gives us a better understanding of the current situation where many teachers and professionals hold strong and opposing opinions about the aims and methods of developing communication and education.

Having set the historical scene, this chapter will then look at the education of deaf children from a view, not based solely on a decision about methodology, but upon decisions based upon the educational, social and linguistic needs of the individual deaf child.

Making Choices

There are always choices to be made concerning any child's education but in the context of the education of deaf children, the concept of choice has an added connotation. Historically there has been, and still is, a great deal of controversy and emotional argument about the variety of approaches used in the education of deaf children. This strongly argued debate centres around the most appropriate mode of communication for deaf children and how this may affect heir educational provision.

Central to this debate is the question of whether or not there is a place for the use of sign language or any sign supported system to help the linguistic development and education of deaf children; or whether their development should be purely through the use of the child's residual hearing and their development of speech.

The past 15 or so years has seen a gradual shift from the polarised positions adopted by many of the educators of deaf children in the past. At the moment, there appears to be a broadening of view. However, many of the issues are far from settled. The roots of this controversy — often referred to as the **oral–manual controversy** — remain firmly planted in a fascinating history of deaf education.

An Historical Perspective

Deaf people have always developed a language of their own, the visual–gestural language of deaf communities called sign language. There have been references to this as early as the fifth century BC. Sign languages have existed as a means of communication, although there is no recording of their potential use in literacy or education. The earliest records of a systematic attempt to educate deaf individuals was in Spain in the 16th century. The honour of being the first teacher of the deaf is often accorded to Pedro Ponce de Leon who undertook the task of teaching the son of a nobleman to read, write and to speak so that he may gain his inheritance. There is no record of his methods but there is a suggestion that he began with reading and writing before moving on to speech and the use of finger spelling. Similarly, in Great Britain in the 18th and 19th centuries teachers were credited with teaching deaf pupils both literacy, and expressive and receptive spoken language skills. Many of the techniques used were kept secret, presumably for financial reasons, and rivalry existed between educators of the deaf.

In France at that time, the Abbe de l'Epee was also working with deaf students but was much less secretive about his methods. His methods were based upon the following principles. First, he believed that sign language was the natural language of the deaf and was their primary vehicle for thought and communication. Using signs from their natural language, he devised a signing system which was able to reflect the grammar of the spoken language. Second, he was influenced by the Spanish teacher, Bonet, who advocated very early intervention in the teaching of deaf children. Third, he believed in a monolingual language environment, that is, only one language used at a time. These thoughts are still consistent with some of the current ideas in the education and linguistic development of deaf children. Although de l'Epee advocated the teaching of articulation skills he felt that the disproportionate amount of time required to teach the spoken word was at the expense of developing the more important intellectual skills. He was heavily criticised for this, particularly by the German school of teachers who were convinced of the value of teaching spoken language to deaf children as a more natural order of learning. Already there was division and argument about methodology among the educators of deaf children. What is interesting is that most of the issues being faced today concerning the education of deaf children have been addressed in previous decades.

Similarly in the United States the need to address the education of deaf children was a concern in the early 1800s when Thomas Gallaudet was chosen to come to Europe to consider the varying methodologies and to decide how best to proceed in the USA. In the event, he found difficulty in accessing the systems in Great Britain and returned to the USA with a French deaf teacher, Laurent Clerc (a pupil of de L'Epee) and introduced methods of communication and education which acknowledged the place of sign language as already established in France. However, the influence from Germany grew in the USA, leading to the introduction of oral methods, with the ensuing debate about methodology (i.e. the oral only method versus the use of sign language).

Gradually **oral methods**, that is teaching deaf children through the spoken language of their society, gained strength and favour in both Europe and in the USA, endorsed by a conference in Milan in 1880, which led to a repression of sign language and an almost total disregard of the place of deaf teachers of deaf children. Methods advocating the use of sign language or a combination of sign and speech became less popular. This legacy of two opposing and hostile camps remained well into the 20th century.

In the 1960s there was a growing awareness both in Europe and in the USA that many deaf children were failing to develop acceptable levels of language skills or to reach their learning potential. It was seen that many deaf children were leaving school with very poor reading and writing skills. The focus of the concern became the 'oral method' then prevalent both in Europe and the USA. It was thought that it was not meeting the needs of many severely and profoundly deaf children. Research, at that time, also indicated that deaf children who had deaf parents and had used sign language from an early age were achieving more highly in school and had more developed literacy skills than other deaf children. This, plus the growing acceptance of sign language as a true and full language, meant there was a shift from a predominantly oral-only approach to one which might include the use of both speech and signs together. This approach was known as **Total Communication** (TC). This term came to mean the use of any method of communication which was effective with deaf children including speech, speech reading, sign, reading and writing. This approach is still prevalent today in many schools. These and other terms will be explored later in the chapter.

More recently, there has been a move towards identifying more clearly the use and role of sign language and the sign systems which support spoken languages and this has led to a more systematic understanding of the use and place of both spoken and signed languages. This identification and separation of sign language and spoken language and their roles in both language acquisition and education has led to the concept of a **bilingual approach** to the language development and education of deaf children which this book addresses.

Currently then the choices facing parents of deaf children falls into three categories or methodologies:

- the oral/aural method,
- total communication,
- the bilingual approach (sign bilingual approach).

In reality, most education authorities or schools have opted for one of these philosophies and developed their education provision for deaf children around that decision. Nevertheless, parents should know of and understand all the possibilities so that they may endeavour to match the educational provision to their own child's needs and wishes.

We will now explore more thoroughly what is entailed in following the various methods

Approaches to Deaf Education

Oral/aural method

This method follows the premise that children's understanding or reception of language should be entirely through use of their residual hearing (aural) and lip reading and the focus for their expressive language should be the spoken language (oral) of their country. The rationale for this approach is that deaf people form a small minority in the hearing community in which they live. It must be a priority for them to be able to communicate with hearing people in their spoken language. This will give the opportunity for a full life within a majority/hearing community of the country in which they live. The primary goal of acquiring speech is justified on the grounds that it gives the deaf person the independence and freedom of choice needed to to participate on equal terms in the wider hearing community.

Most deaf children do have some residual hearing, however small, and with the early diagnosis of deafness and the consistent use of sophisticated hearing aids, developing the use of this residual hearing is a priority. The development of spoken language is through hearing and speech alone with emphasis placed upon listening skills and the development of speech and lip reading. This requires considerable effort and concentration on the part of the child, and while the additional use of sign language may well ease this communicative act, it is considered by oralists to detract from the early development of speech. Therefore in an oral/aural approach to the language development and education of deaf children, there is no place for the use of any form of signed communication.

Total communication

The Total Communication approach was developed as a result of research evidence which suggested that, for some deaf children, the exclusive use of spoken language failed to provide sufficient linguistic input at the crucial time for language development. Total Communication is considered to give the maximum opportunity for a deaf child to have access to a range of communication options appropriate to their individual needs. These options range from those based on spoken languages (i.e. use of speech, amplified residual hearing, lip reading, gestures, reading, writing and the use of sign support systems) to the use of sign language.

The most common interpretation of a total communication approach is the use of spoken language simultaneously with a signed version of all (Signed English) or a part (Sign Supported English) of the utterance. The justification for this is that if deaf children are exposed to spoken language and sign-supported communication simultaneously (Sim-Com), then the inclusion of a visual, signed element will enhance their understanding of the spoken word and so contribute to the development of the spoken language. The disadvantage of this system is that it has proved difficult to match the spoken word accurately with the signed part and therefore might, in the end, be confusing for the deaf child.

Bilingual approach

The rationale for a bilingual approach is that many deaf children, if exposed to sign language, would readily develop it as a first or preferred language at the most appropriate age in their linguistic development. It is regarded as their right to have the opportunity to acquire good skills in sign language as a first language. This will help with cognitive development and also to develop English skills at a later time. The use of sign language also allows a deaf child the opportunity to mix with deaf children and adults if they so wish. It is thought that this opportunity helps children to develop a positive identity for themselves as deaf children

The bilingual approach responds to some of the limitations of the total communication approach discussed earlier, by acknowledging the place and use of sign language as the natural language of the deaf community and its place in the communicative, intellectual and educational development of deaf children. The importance of English, both as the language of the wider social community and the language of reading and writing (literacy), is fully acknowledged and must be learnt by deaf children, but as a separate or second language.

The term **sign bilingualism** is used when the two languages involved are a signed language and a spoken/written language.

By-passing the Debate or an Alternative View

Having considered very briefly the historical context and also a short outline of the ensuing debate, it is now possible to think of the 'debate' not as a mutually exclusive choice, but as offering options. For many deaf children, particularly those with a slight or moderate hearing loss, an oral/aural approach is completely appropriate, just as appropriate as an early introduction to sign language is for profoundly deaf children. So the matter of choice is not about which method to choose *per se* but which option is most appropriate for which child. There is a growing conviction that within a sign bilingual approach the range of options, responding to the varying needs of all categories deaf children, can be addressed.

We now return again to the earlier discussion of the deaf child within a *linguistic model* with individual linguistic needs (see Chapter 2). Having established the deaf child's first or preferred language then those children for whom English is their first and preferred language, an approach which continues to develop these skills is clearly the most appropriate. For children who are developing sign language as a first language it is vital that their early access to sign language continues into their school experience. Then the issue of learning English as a second language must be addressed. For those children an approach which incorporates both languages would be the most suitable path to follow. The choice of school must reflect the linguistic needs of the child.

However, as most deaf children do not fall neatly into these two above categories, it is more appropriate to think of them as somewhere along a *continuum* of communicative and educational need with a diverse range of needs falling between these two extremes. So rather than continue to debate the merits of one method over another, it becomes more appropriate to put that energy into careful assessment of the individual **child's linguistic and educational needs** and aim to meet those needs in the most appropriate educational setting.

Decisions about Educational Placement

Before decisions can be made about a school there are many basic factors that must be taken into account such as where you live, the child's own skills as well as aspects to do with the school. A placement (eventually decided upon by parents and professionals together) will reflect an awareness and an informed and balanced consideration of all these.

The overriding considerations when discussing suitable placement are:

(1) an assessment of the individual needs of the child including language development, social skills and learning skills;
(2) the implications of including deaf children in mainstream school;
(3) the type of additional support available in the school; and
(4) the implications of including deaf children in Special Schools.

Each of these issues will now be considered in more detail.

Assessing the individual needs of the child

The needs of each child may be divided into the following three areas which are enlarged upon in the following sections.

Language needs consist of:

- the need to continue to develop receptive and expressive skills in their first or preferred language to a level appropriate with their age,
- the need to continue to develop English as a second language if appropriate and
- the opportunity to communicate successfully with peers and adults, both socially and academically, in the school setting.

Social needs consist of:
- an acceptance by the school as valued members of the whole school setting;
- the communicative competence to relate equally to peers and adults,
- the ability to develop positive relationships with peers and adults; and
- the opportunity to develop social and functional independence skills.

Learning needs consist of:
- an expectation that the deaf child will reach its full academic potential,
- the opportunity to develop independent learning skills,
- the same opportunities to access the curriculum of the school as fully as their hearing peers.

Some deaf children have difficulties in addition to their deafness. The needs of these children should be viewed with the same criteria as children who are deaf with no additional difficulties. However, it is vital to ensure that needs arising from these additional difficulties are also being assessed and are met either in the mainstream or in a special school.

Deaf children in mainstream schools

The trend towards including deaf children into mainstream schools was reinforced in England by the Warnock Report (DES, 1978) and the following government legislation in (DES, 1981). A current estimate is that some 80% of deaf children are in mainstream education with varying degrees and types of support. Some 10% are in special schools and the remaining 10% are either of pre-school age and having support from the local education authority, or in further or higher education. The rationale for the inclusion of deaf children (or any child perceived as having special educational needs) is that mainstream school, by adapting the curriculum and providing appropriate support, should be able to meet the educational needs of all children. This then offers children with additional needs, including deaf children, the opportunity to have the same curriculum as their peers. The mainstream school setting allows all children to remain part of their local community and associate with their friends both in and out of school.

This move to include deaf children in mainstream school, wherever possible, has led to many special schools for deaf children closing. This has meant that the remaining schools have tended to specialise, addressing, for example, the needs of deaf children who have difficulties in addition to their deafness.

The Warnock Report assumed that there would be varying types or levels of integration for deaf children (and all children with special needs) under the following three headings:

- **Locational integration** — deaf children would be receiving their education in the mainstream school
- **Social integration** — deaf children would play alongside, eat alongside and generally socialise with peers in the playground.
- **Functional integration** — deaf children would learn alongside their peers in regular classes for all or part of the time.

Deaf children are fully integrated into the mainstream school when they are participating in all the three of these areas. Then they are on an equal footing with their hearing peers. While the integration of the vast majority of deaf children is appropriate, it is important to ensure that the fullest possible integration in these terms, is achieved. This is through specialist support and curriculum differentiation. To this end, there is a need to ensure that deaf children will benefit *socially* and *emotionally* and *academically* from their placement in a mainstream school. The mainstream school must be prepared to address these issues as part of the whole school ethos.

For deaf children to benefit **socially and emotionally** the school should:

- positively address the issue of the school as a social setting for deaf children;
- ensure that deaf children are not socially isolated either in the classroom or the wider school environment;
- provide opportunities for essential social learning both in the classroom and in the wider school context; and
- encourage social and functional independence.

To benefit **academically** the school should:

- have appropriate expectations of deaf children;
- offer enhanced provision of appropriate resources to promote learning;
- promote independent learning skills;
- ensure all staff are aware of the implications of deaf children in the school and classroom; and
- ensure all areas of the curriculum are available to deaf children through appropriate support.

What support should be provided in a mainstream school

To ensure that deaf children are well supported in mainstream schools it is important for all the staff of the school to have:

- a positive attitude to having deaf children in their school,
- an awareness of the language and cultural issues important to the deaf,
- full information about deafness and the implications for the deaf child in the classroom,
- experience of meting deaf adults and other relevant professionals and
- the knowledge that meeting the deaf children's educational needs is a collaborative one between them and the additional support staff.

The amount and type of additional specialist support should reflect the specific needs of the individual child. This support would fall along a **continuum of provision** which should be flexible enough to meet the child's **continuum of need** and to reflect the changing needs of deaf children over time.

At one end of this **continuum of provision** are deaf children who are taught in the local mainstream school alongside their hearing peers, unsupported or with little support. These deaf children are likely to be those with well developed English as a first language. At the other end of the continuum, there are those children who have developed sign language as their first and preferred language. These children may need full-time specialist support from teachers of the deaf. Communication support workers and notetakers should also be available to ensure that deaf children have the same opportunities in the classroom as their mainstream peers.

Most deaf children, of course, do not fall neatly into these two options and it becomes a matter of an appropriate and flexible range of support to suit each child.

The support available within a local mainstream school could include some of the following options. Children placed in a mainstream school in either of the following categories are likely to have spoken English as their first language and will function in that language for their entire school careers:

- *Individual placement in a class in the local mainstream school* with monitoring and advice from a visiting teacher of the deaf but no direct in-class support to either the child or the mainstream teacher.
- *Individual placement in a class in the local mainstream school* with some direct support in the classroom for the deaf child and teacher for some of the time. The support will be from visiting teachers and possibly other professionals depending on the degree and type of need.

The type of specialist support in the next two categories may vary depending upon the philosophy of the local authority:

- *Placement in a class in a selected mainstream school* with other deaf children and specialist staff working permanently in the school alongside mainstream teachers. *Children may have additional support in the classroom and also the possibility of withdrawal from mainstream classes for extra tuition appropriate to the needs of the child.*
- *Placement in a unit attached to a mainstream school* where the support is predominantly in a separate class for deaf children taught by specialist staff but with the option to integrate into mainstream classes for appropriate curriculum areas.

In an authority where the philosophy is an oral one then the support to the child and their access to the curriculum will be through English regardless of the child's degree of deafness or preferred first language. Within a Total Communication philosophy the range of specialist support offered to the child will be from Sign Language, Manually Coded English to English depending on the needs of the child and the demands of the teaching situation.

Special schools for deaf children

The special school or the school for the deaf providing segregated education for deaf children, is a school which is separate from the mainstream school and brings together deaf children of all ages in one setting. Such schools may be residential or day schools, many of them being a mixture of both. The special school has an important place in the 'continuum of provision' for deaf children as it offers an environment where deaf children have all their educational input from specialist staff (teachers of the deaf and subject specialist teachers). They are also part of a community with all deaf peers and, depending upon the philosophy of the school, deaf adults. In this regard, it is important to appreciate the role of special schools for the deaf in relation to the development and personal identity of deaf children and their part in the deaf community of the school.

The type of staff in the school will depend upon the school's philosophy. A school with a strong oral philosophy will have specialist teachers of the deaf, subject specialists and speech therapists and the use of spoken and written English will be the mode in which formal education is delivered. Children are likely to experience the use of sign language in the social setting of the school.

In a school with a Total Communication philosophy, where deaf children will be developing both sign language and English, the staff will consist of both deaf and hearing adults. The deaf adults are particularly important as deaf role models and fluent users of sign language.

Implications of Different Educational Settings

Mainstream schools

A summary of the issues schools should address and the type of support deaf children may expect in different educational settings follows. It includes the additional support offered by a school with a total communication philosophy. The support has been identified in terms of social, linguistic and academic needs of the deaf child. This information is set out in two columns:

(1) Support available in all mainstream schools providing for deaf children plus those resourced schools with an **oral/aural** philosophy;

(2) Additional support in resourced schools with a **total communication/ bilingual philosophy.**

Oral/aural settings	*Total communication settings*
Socially children will have:	*Socially* children will have:
• the opportunity to interact with peers from the locality and wider social environment; • the opportunity to participate in extra curricular activities with hearing peers; • the opportunity to develop the independence skills required to function effectively in the hearing community; • the possibility of social isolation within the school setting.	• the opportunity to socialise with deaf and hearing peer group; • the opportunity to have regular contact with deaf adults; • the opportunity to participate in extra curricular activities with deaf and hearing peers.

Oral/aural settings	*Total communication settings*
Academically children will have	*Academically* children will have
• the opportunity to access the same curriculum as hearing peers; • equivalent teacher expectation of deaf and hearing children; • the same assessment opportunities and criteria as their hearing peers; • the opportunity to develop independent learning skills.	• the opportunity to access the curriculum through a first or preferred language; • the opportunity to have interpretation into a first language in the classroom; • examination and assessment procedures delivered in a first language; • appropriate resources and support in the classroom, i.e. notetakers.
Linguistically the children will have:	*Linguistically* the children will have:
• the language of the school environment and education which is spoken and written English; • opportunities to continue to develop the first language in the natural environment.	• opportunities to continue to develop first language skills; • opportunities to develop English as a second language.
Specialist support in addition to mainstream staff will be in the form of a *visiting teacher of the deaf* whose role is:	*Specialist support* in addition to mainstream staff will be in the form of a *teacher of the deaf* whose role is:
• to liaise with and advise mainstream staff; • to offer some direct support to the child in the classroom or additional tutorial support; • to give appropriate back-up for audiological requirements; • to encourage and maintain home school links.	• to support access to the mainstream curriculum; • to develop English language skills; • to ensure appropriate back-up for audiological requirements; • to encourage and maintenance of home school links.
	Deaf adults whose role is:
	• to continue to develop sign language skills; • to be a role model for both deaf and hearing members of the school; • to enhance access to the curriculum by introducing new concepts in a child's first language.
	Communication support workers/educational interpreters and notetakers whose role is:
	• to facilitate access to the curriculum of the school where appropriate.

The implications for the deaf child in any type of mainstream placement depends upon the communication philosophy of the education authority. If the authority has an oral philosophy the nature of the support both linguistically and academically will be similar to that offered to children who are individually integrated into the mainstream school, although greater in intensity. The major advantages of a Total Communication philosophy are that it offers a wide range of communication options to meet the needs of all deaf children and the placement of more than one deaf child in a school would redress the possible feelings of isolation felt by some deaf children.

Schools for the deaf

Oral/aural settings	*Total communication settings*
A child placed in a school for the deaf with a strong oral philosophy will experience spoken and written English as a form of communication in the academic setting of the school.	In a school for the deaf with a total communication, bilingual philosophy, the deaf child will experience communications ranging from English and sign supported systems to sign language in both the educational and social setting of the school.
The teaching will usually be exclusively by specialist teachers of the deaf and subject specialist teachers.	The teaching will usually be exclusively by specialist teachers of the deaf and subject specialist teachers.
There will be other involved professionals such as speech therapists.	There will be other involved professionals such as speech therapists. It is to be expected that all teachers will have well developed sign language skills and that deaf adults will have a role, both as deaf role models and in the development of the sign language skills of the children.

Case Histories

The following are descriptions of a variety of deaf children and their school experiences. They are based upon the true reflections of families who feel confident that their deaf child is receiving their education in an appropriate setting and both they and the child are happy with the situation.

MICHAEL is 5 years old. He is the youngest of three boys. His parents and his two brothers are all hearing. He has a *mild conductive hearing loss* in the order of 40 dB.

He is beginning to make good use of his listening skills and his hearing aids. Although he has some difficulty in following what people are saying unless he is looking at them, he is developing spoken English as his preferred language. He does not hear all the quieter sounds of speech and this is reflected in his spoken language where he tends to miss the ends of words and some of the quieter parts of speech such as the unvoiced consonant sounds such as s, sh, f, th. This can make his speech a little difficult to understand until you are familiar with him and the context of the conversation.

Michael now attends the same local primary school as his two brothers where he has settled in well. All the teachers there knew him before and were all prepared to support him in attending his local school.

He is now in a Year 1 class of 28 children where he has some additional support from a visiting teacher of the deaf. The teacher does extra tutorial work with Michael mostly to ensure that he is developing appropriate literacy and numeracy skills. He is also responsible for monitoring Michael's progress and continually assessing the appropriateness of the school setting. Equally importantly, he has liaised with all the teachers in the school who are now familiar with the issues of having a deaf child in their school and in their class. They are familiar with the management of his hearing aids, how to optimise the acoustic conditions of the classroom and appropriate seating positions for Michael in the classroom. Michael also visits a speech therapist who has developed an individual program for further developing and assessing his spoken language skills.

Michael has settled in well into the school and has several hearing friends in the class. His parents are very happy with the situation although they appreciate that it was helped by the fact that he was already familiar with the school and they with him. They feel that the support from the teacher of the deaf is very important both to support Michael's work and to assess his progress and they appreciate the continuing contact they have with him and the school.

They are a little unhappy about the fact that he is the only child in the school who is deaf and feel he misses the deaf friends he had made through pre-school support groups.

SUSAN is 13 years old and she has one younger and one older brother. They and her parents are hearing. She has a *severe sensori-neural hearing loss* in the order of 70–75 dB.

She makes good use of her hearing aids in school although she prefers not to wear them at home. In the early years her parents preferred to encourage the use of spoken English although they did support their communication with her by using some signs supporting their speech. Susan has developed spoken English as a first language although her articulation is not very clear and her vocabulary is relatively limited in comparison to hearing peers. She has well developed literacy and numeracy skills but still has some difficulty in understanding new concepts in the broader areas of the curriculum.

Susan now attends a residential school for the deaf which has an oral/aural philosophy where the curriculum is delivered through English and there is an emphasis on developing spoken language. She is in a class of seven children. She is taught by teachers of the deaf and there are a wide range of specialist subjects on the curriculum.

Susan is well settled in the school and enjoys the social interaction with other deaf children both in and out of the classroom. She enjoys coming home for the weekends and holidays but does not have many hearing friends in the locality. Communication with her family is good as they all understand her quite well but she does have difficulty with hearing peers.

Susan's parents are pleased that she seems to be happy in school and feel that the environment is caring and suits Susan's needs. They regret the fact that it is so far away and they feel that they do not have the contact with the school or the other parents as they do with their hearing children in the local school. They feel that she is sometimes lonely at home and regret the fact that her deaf school friends are widely scattered.

JEREMY is 9 years old and is *profoundly deaf.* He has one sister who is also profoundly deaf as is his father. His mother is partially hearing. All the family have well developed sign language skills although his mother also uses spoken English.

Jeremy had developed BSL as his first language although he does use some English with his mother. His articulation is not at all clear although he has well formed lip patterns. He does not like his hearing aids although he will wear them in school if specially requested. Through his hearing aids he is likely to hear a limited and distorted pattern of speech although he will be aware of most environmental sounds. He is at his most relaxed when communicating in BSL and that is the language through which he can most easily access the school curriculum.

Jeremy is on the roll of a large resourced mainstream primary school where he is taught by both deaf and hearing adults. There are about 20 deaf children spread across the age ranges throughout the school. He is in a class of 32 children in Year 5. He has the same opportunity to access the curriculum as his hearing peers in the school. In this he is supported in the classroom by a teacher of the deaf who is responsible for planning his individual education programme and for appropriately differentiating the teaching resources. They are also responsible for developing his English skills, both written and spoken. Sometimes he is withdrawn from the classroom to work in a small group of deaf children on particular aspects of the curriculum. The support from deaf adults for Jeremy would be to continue to develop his BSL skills and to ensure that initial concepts are presented in his first language and other areas of discussion are explored.

Although it is a mainstream school and Jeremy is in a class with hearing peers he prefers to work and play mostly with the other deaf children in the school. He also seems to relate more closely to the teachers of the deaf and the deaf adults in the school. He very much enjoys the opportunity to be part of the out-of-school activities, particularly being in the football team.

Jeremy's parents are delighted with the progress that he is making in school. Both of them had been to a residential school for the deaf and they were initially worried about placing Jeremy in a mainstream school as they had no personal experience of one. The fact that he is at school with some other deaf children pleases them. They are sorry that the mainstream school is not a local one as this means that Jeremy has very few friends around him at home. At first they were very concerned that he would have to go to school in a taxi every day but theses fears have now subsided as he grows up.

USHA is 10 years old and she *has a moderate hearing loss in the order of 65 dB*. Her parents are hearing and the first language of the home is Urdu. She has an older brother and sister who are both hearing and who speak both Urdu and English which has been learned mostly from school. Usha's mother speaks Urdu and her English skills are not well developed. However she goes regularly to the Asian mothers support group where she has been learning some sign language which she uses with Usha. They communicate effectively with some spoken Urdu and some use of signs. Usha is struggling to use three languages. Her preferred mode of communication would be a spoken language but with the dual spoken languages at home and in school she finds some use of sign language is an effective back up for her communication. None of her potential communication skills are developed to an age appropriate level and this causes some frustration both for Usha and her family. Usha wears her hearing aids in school but she does not like using them at home.

Usha attends her local primary school. Her parents wanted her to be in a school with other Asian, Urdu-speaking children and this was a priority for them despite the possible difficulties with her developing linguistic skills. Usha has up to half a day a week of specialist support from a visiting teacher of the deaf and she and her family also have support from a bilingual family support worker. The school curriculum is delivered in English.

Usha's progress is continually monitored by the staff of the mainstream school and the support teacher of the deaf.

Usha and her family are pleased with the current situation although they appreciate that if she experiences difficulty in managing then a move to a school where there would be the possibility of further developing her sign language skills is an option.

It can be seen from the case studies that the issues of placement are not particularly straightforward and there are always additional individual factors related to each child and their family. Having decided upon a placement there will still be advantages and disadvantages to each one both in relation to the educational setting and in terms of the communication philosophy of the authority. It is important for parents to ensure that they are fully informed of all the considerations and then for them to feel confident and empowered to make informed choices in partnership with involved professionals.

Conclusion

Any school or education authority which has one fixed approach to the communication and academic needs of the deaf child will be unlikely to be able to meet the needs of all the deaf children. This is significant in the issue of the rights of the deaf child to have equal access to the same educational opportunities as their hearing peers. It is important to reiterate the original premise that the focus should be on the continuum appropriately to meet those individual needs. The focus should not be on the methodological debate which is still giving rise to the constraint on individual choices and decisions that many parents and professionals have to make. The special or mainstream schools most equipped to meet those needs will be those who recognise and can meet the linguistic, social and academic needs of each individual child.

Summary

The choice of school placement is a significant and important area. It is really only through some understanding of the choices and the implication of those choices, that parents can hope to have an informed view.

The general principles guiding the choice of placement are:

- each child's specific needs are of prime importance;
- carefull assessment must be made of their needs;
- needs should be continually assessed and expected to change over time; and
- appropriate resources and support should be flexible to meet those needs.

Additional Reading

Gregory, S., Knight, P., McCracken, W., Powers, S. and Watson, L. (eds) (1998) *Issues in Deaf Education*. London: Fulton Press.
 Chapters 2.3, 2.4 and 2.5 all carefully consider the options presented within deaf education including the oral/aural method, Total Communication and sign bilingualism

Marschark, M. (1997) *Raising and Educating a Deaf Child*. Oxford: Oxford University Press.
 Chapter 6 entitled 'Going to School' covers many of the issues which parents should consider. Although it is focused on the USA the issues remain very relevant for children in the UK.

Chapter 9
Finding Your Way Around the System

Introduction

The aims of this chapter are to introduce you to some of the terminology, jargon and names you will hear in your dealings with hospitals, schools and social services. Also to explain how some of the systems work, which you will inevitably meet as a family with a deaf child. The following relates to systems in the UK but there is evidence to suggest that very similar processes are in place in other parts of the world, particularly in the USA.

Knowing your way around 'the system' is a phrase we very often hear in everyday life. It may be the system required to obtain a house, to have a telephone installed or to reclaim the money from overpaid bills. The new or previously unknown 'systems' the family of a deaf child may find themselves part of are the medical system, the education system and the social system. In other words there will be links with hospitals, schools and possibly other services. Many parents have commented that being involved in so many systems and the related professionals is overwhelming and unhelpful. They feel that they often receive conflicting and unhelpful advice.

> With Ben I started off confident about how to take care of him . . . then suddenly this battery of professionals has arrived on the scene and in a sense, my child, the one I know and love, has been taken away and a new one substituted. (Lorraine Fletcher, 1987: 30)

The more knowledge you have of these areas the more confident you will be in them. This will enable you to select and benefit from the support offered in a way that most helps you.

> If you don't know how school hierarchies, medical teams, or other organisations work you can easily misinterpret what happens. (Freeman *et al.*, 1981: 267)

Relevant Government Acts

It is helpful for parents to have an understanding of relevant government policy because hospitals, schools, social services and the related professionals usually come under government and local authority control and, as such, have to respond to government acts, papers and recommendations. The government is constantly assessing and reviewing their policies and some of the following are the most important in the area of support for children with special needs.

The *1989 Children Act* (Department of Health, 1989) addressed the issue of the number of services and professionals involved with deaf children and those with special needs in two ways . One was that all the support services involved with children with special needs should work together to provide a cooperative type of support to families with various agencies, i.e. medical, educational and social services working together. Second, there was emphasis in the Act on the development of services which are responsive to the views of children and their parents when establishing the type of support needed. So, in essence, the Children Act protects the needs and rights of the child and expects local authorities to promote shared initiatives between all the services involved in supporting children with special needs.

The phrase 'children with special needs' was established in another government *1981 Education Act*. Previously, children had been identified by having a specific category of handicap. This may have been deafness, blindness physical handicap, mental handicap and others. This 1981 Act describes children's handicaps in terms of their individual **'Special Educational Need'** (SEN*)*. In essence a child is considered to have a special educational need if he or she has learning difficulties significantly greater then those of other children of the same age or has a disability which affects access to the educational facilities which are generally provided.

The other important outcome of this 1981 Education Act was the emphasis on the fact that children with special educational needs should, as far as possible, be educated in the mainstream school with other children of a similar age. The term 'integration' of pupils with SEN was an outcome of this Act.

To ensure that the educational needs all children with special educational needs are identified, and that appropriate support is given in mainstream schools, a form of assessment was devised. As a result of this assessment a **Statement of Special Educational Needs** is produced for each child. This identifies the specific needs of each individual child and outlines ways in which these needs are to be supported in schools.

The 1981 Act has now been superseded by the *Education Act 1993* which held on to the spirit of the previous Act but strengthened the roles and rights of parents in the assessment of and subsequent support for their children. The 1993 Act also stated that all schools were required by law to have written policies for addressing the issues related to special educational needs within their particular school.

In 1994, the *Code of Practice* (COP) established a set of guidelines for identifying and supporting children with special educational needs. In particular these identify the points (called stages) at which local authorities and schools must carefully plan the support for children with special educational needs. As a result of this careful assessment an **Individual Education Plan** (IEP) should be produced for all children with special educational needs. Schools should also establish a post within the school or a teacher with special responsibility for all Special Educational Needs provision within the school . This person is called the **Special Needs Co-ordinator** (SENCO). The *Code of Practice* reinforces the role of parents in assessing and devising support for their own children, advocates close cooperation between the agencies working together and remains supportive of integration for all children with SEN.

The latest government initiative in response to the needs of children with Special Educational Needs is the *Green Paper 1997 Excellence for All — Meeting Special Educational Needs*. This is, at the moment, a consultation paper which means that it is not yet a legal document. However, the document reinforces the idea that all children with special educational needs should be educated in mainstream schools. With the aim of increasing the level and quality of support in mainstream schools, the expression integration has broadened into 'inclusion'. The paper does reflect the fact that, for some children, inclusion as unquestioning placement in a mainstream school may not always be appropriate. For those children specialist provision in special schools will be maintained and enhanced.

Making the System Work for You

Once your child has been diagnosed as having a hearing loss you will inevitably be drawn into this variety of systems which are interlinked and all have a very specific role in supporting the family. They are there to work for you although the number of people and situations you are suddenly confronted with may feel quite overwhelming. There follows a general description of the way these systems work, although clearly there will be variations in different areas.

The medical system

Deafness is usually discovered in one of two ways. Parents may be uneasy about their child and suspect they are not hearing well or responding well to sound. For others it may be at the **routine screening test** for hearing carried out by **health visitors** in the home or at the baby clinic at the local General Practitioners (GP) surgery. In either situation it is the GP who is the first port of call and if deafness is suspected the doctor will refer you to the **Ear Nose and Throat** (ENT) surgeon at the local hospital.

It is at the hospital that further hearing tests will be carried out in the **Audiology Clinic**. This often requires several visits which, although frustrating for parents, allows for a variety of tests to be carried out by **audiological scientists** to diagnose the precise nature of the hearing loss. It is at this clinic that appropriate hearing aids are prescribed and usually fitted. The audiology clinic is responsible for the ongoing assessment of hearing loss and maintenance of hearing aids. Links with the audiology clinic and the ENT department of the hospital will be ongoing throughout a child's school days and beyond. This is to ensure that appropriate hearing aids are always available and that the medical condition of the ear is carefully monitored.

In many places a close link is made and maintained between paediatric audiology and educational services for deaf children. A **Teacher of the Deaf** (TOD) will very often be present at the clinic when diagnosis is made and can set up contact with you from that point.

The education system

Pre-school and nursery

Most areas provide support to parents from the time when their child is diagnosed as deaf and there is widespread collaboration between local education services for deaf children and paediatric audiology services. This support is usually from a Teacher of the Deaf and their initial role is to reinforce and explain information given at the time of diagnosis which may not have been clearly 'heard'.

> I didn't agree with the ENT consultant's diagnosis of profound deafness and the TOD was a great comfort, talking and listening and explaining to us. (Parent in conversation)

The Teacher of the Deaf is there to support the parents through the next few months and should have information in all the following areas. They have a key role in giving information and providing opportunities in any of these areas. For example, they can give information on:

- hearing aids and how to encourage their use,
- the nature of deafness and the implications of the loss for language and educational development,
- the variety of communication options open to the child and family,
- aspects of social and educational development,
- possible educational placements,
- related government legislation and
- other sources of support.

Alternatively they can provide the following opportunities for:

- an introduction to a deaf adult working for the service who can discuss what it means to be deaf and introduce families to the option of sign language,
- to observe a deaf adult communicating with their child in sign language,
- the chance to learn the basics of sign language,
- to meet with other parents with deaf children,
- to meet with a range of professionals involved with the child and discuss problems.

You should use this opportunity to gather as much information for yourselves as possible. This will give you confidence to make informed decisions about your own child and to be part of a team with professionals and not daunted by them. *Parents as Partners* is a phrase that is often used.

> All to often parents describe 'losing' their child to he professionals, as the number of people with an interest in the child suddenly grows. (Robinson, 1991: 98)

Early-years education

The next step in the educational process to be addressed by both parents and professionals is the possibility of going to nursery or playgroup. Depending upon your child's language development there are a range of options. It may be a local playgroup or a deaf playgroup where children can play and communicate with other deaf and hearing children and their parents. This also gives an opportunity for parents to share ideas and information amongst themselves and share mutual concerns. The teacher of the deaf should have full information about the playgroup options in your area.

By the time your child is three there will be the option for them to go into an **Educational Nursery**. They may go there on an assessment basis where full observations and assessment of their needs can be carried out. In some places this assessment is carried out before the child goes to nursery. Either way the assessment is likely to involve a further range of professionals including **Educational Psychologist**, Teacher of the Deaf, **Speech Therapist** and possibly others. This may seem overwhelming but it does assure a 'multi-disciplinary approach' to assessment that should give a full and balanced view of your child and their particular needs. Of course you also have a full part to play in the assessment of your child and the decision about their placement. This relatively early assessment is crucial to the planning and preparation for transition into appropriate full-time education. The final assessment in this process becomes the **Statement of Special Educational Need**.

All nurseries, including those with deaf children, work within a pre-national curriculum framework called '**Desirable Outcomes for Nursery**' where they address the learning needs of young children in the following areas which include social skills, communicative skills and their general experience of the environment.

Full-time school — primary

It may be appropriate for your deaf child to go to his/her local mainstream school. If this is the case then there may be extra support in the school for them. Depending upon the particular need the child may have extra help from someone within the school in addition to the class teacher. This is usually a **Special Needs Assistant** or, in some circumstances, it is a **Communication Support Worker**. This is someone who supports a child whose first language is not the same as the classroom. In the case of a deaf child that language will be sign language.

Many deaf children go to a **Resourced School** which is a mainstream school where many of the deaf children in the area go. The school will be additionally resourced to meet the needs of the deaf children within the school. These additional resources are usually Teachers of the Deaf, deaf adults often called **Deaf Instructors,** Communication Support Workers with additional input from speech therapists and educational audiologists. The educational audiologists work with the education service and their role is to maintain all hearing aids etc. in optimum working order in relation to the home and school environment.

Within the first term of starting at primary school teachers conduct a **Baseline Assessment** on all children which aims to arrive at an understanding of the child's general development on entering school so as to assess their subsequent progress realistically.

Most deaf children will have a statement of educational need when they enter full-time school. From this statement teachers will prepare an **Individual Education Programme** (IEP) which identifies the particular learning and social needs of each child. Children may also have an **Individual Audiological Profile** (IAP) which identifies particular strategies in relation to the use of hearing aids and the development of residual hearing.

A child's statement is reviewed at least once a year and possibly more frequently if parents or anyone involved with the child feels it is appropriate. This **Annual Review** comprises a meeting of all involved professionals, parents and special needs coordinator to review the suitability of the placement, the progress of the child and also to set specific learning targets for the coming term or year.

SEN Tribunals were set up in 1993 as an independent body whose role is to arbitrate between parents and Local Education Authorities (LEAs) where there is disagreement between parents and the authority about the most suitable support and educational placement for their child. Their task is to decide what is in the best interests of the child at the time of the hearing. It is not to reflect on complaints about previous support.

Most deaf children who are in a mainstream primary school will be part of the usual classes in the school and, where appropriate, they will learn alongside the hearing children in that class. The extra support for them may be in the form of a specialist teacher in the classroom to provide additional help. Sometimes support is given outside the classroom in small groups of children or on a one-to-one basis.

All the children in the school, both deaf and hearing, will be following the **National Curriculum** which has been in place since 1988. The National Curriculum gives a framework, outlining what children are entitled to be taught. It covers 'core' subjects, which are English, maths and science and other 'foundation' subjects such as history, geography etc. The National Curriculum has three **Key Stages** with an assessment at the end of each stage. These assessments are called **Standard Assessment Tasks** (SATs) and occur when children are 7, 11, 14 and **General Certificates of Secondary Education** at 16 years of age. Teachers of the Deaf will have information on the most appropriate ways of administering these tests for all deaf pupils so that they are not disadvantaged. Appropriate modifications should be made to the National Curriculum through a child's statement. **Teacher Assessments** of children are evidence collected by the teacher which complements the results of the SATs.

British Sign Language and Standard Assessment Tasks. Teachers of the Deaf working with bilingual deaf children are developing parallel Standard Assessment Tasks in British Sign Language which can be delivered through the child's first language. The guidelines are based on input from a working party of Teachers of the Deaf who specialise in working with children. In fact all standardised assessment tasks have specific guidelines for children with special educational needs.

A **National Literacy Hour** (and a numeracy hour) has been recently introduced by the UK government in response to the perceived poor standards of literacy and numeracy in schools. This means that for an hour per day the whole class will address specific issues to do with developing reading and writing skills. Again it will be the role of the support teacher to ensure that the deaf children have appropriate support for this time in the classroom. This only applies to primary schools.

Full-time school — secondary

Entering secondary education can be a daunting prospect for any child. Children are usually moving from a small establishment with a small number of children and fewer staff to a relatively large secondary school. Generally, in a primary school, teachers know most of the children in the school and vice versa and children are very familiar with the layout of the building. Primary school children are usually with one teacher for most subjects. Many primary schools do aim to give the children learning experiences, similar to those they will encounter in the secondary school, before they leave.

Secondary schools, in contrast, are large buildings with many more pupils and staff. Pupils are more likely to know their year head and pupils within their own school year than the head of the school or other members of staff. The style of learning is different in that it is subject based with different members of staff for each subject. Pupils are expected to move around the school to different classrooms for different subjects. They are expected to find their own way to lunch; the way of being ushered around as a class as in the primary school hardly ever happens.

Usually secondary schools who have several deaf children in them have a '**base**' where the deaf pupils may have specialised tuition and can also congregate socially. Occasionally it is said that a base discourages deaf pupils from interacting with the hearing pupils in the school. For all deaf children, whether they use sign language or spoken English as their preferred language the opportunity to get together and relax socially is very important. The opportunities for spending time with hearing pupils in the secondary school is more often linked to common interests such as sport or drama. Common interests provide a link where deaf/hearing friendships and relationships can be forged and should be encouraged by all people within the school.

Within the secondary school the focus of all support should be to enable deaf pupils to access the national curriculum as delivered in the school. Deaf pupils should have equal access with their hearing peers. The type of support provided for them should aim to interpret the curriculum as it is delivered to all pupils. This means that there will be qualified **Sign Language Interpreters** or **Communication Support Workers** in the classroom for pupils who would most easily understand the curriculum through sign language; also teachers of the deaf whose role is to ensure that the curriculum is appropriately delivered for deaf pupils. They will also have responsibility for ensuring that the English skills of all pupils are developed to the individual pupil's capacity. Teachers of the Deaf will offer specialist advice with regard to appropriate modifications to formal examinations, both internal and external.

The social services system

The third system which most families of deaf children come across is that linked to social support. There is often a misunderstanding about the role of the social support system for the families of deaf children. There is a misconception which is that if a family is offered support from any form of social services then they must be in some way failing. This is not true and especially not true for the families of deaf children. You should expect to be introduced to a **Social Worker with Deaf People** early on. They will be able to tell you about such matters as any financial support you can claim, both for the parents as carers and for older deaf children. They are often linked with the local **Deaf Club** and are involved in organising play schemes and youth clubs. It is important for you to know what is available so that you can take advantage of the service as and when you required.

The **National Deaf Children's Society** is 'working for all deaf children' and provides support advice and information on all aspects of deafness. Their function is also as an independent advocate for the deaf child and his/her family in that they are a society that works closely with both education and social services but is independent of both. The society works through a large network of local groups with both regional staff and a national office in London.

Conclusion

When considering the three main systems affecting the families of deaf children and all the personnel working within them, it is hardly surprising that parents feel overwhelmed by the number of professionals who become involved with them. For this reason it is important that families are clear about the function of each of the services. They can then identify for themselves that person who is the link or key person who can be the consistent coordinator of all support offered. In reality this person is usually the Teacher of the Deaf involved with the family because they are the natural bridge between medicine, social services and education.

Summary

It is accepted that parents of deaf children will meet a lot of professional people and become involved in the various systems which provide support and help to the families of deaf children. It is a fact of life this invariably means coming to terms with the technical terms and the 'jargon' used to describe much of what goes on in these systems. In this chapter we have considered:

- the medical system,
- the education system and
- the social services system.

Parents' knowledge of the systems ensures that they are able to fully access them and to feel confident when they are inevitably placed in situations where these terms are used freely.

Additional Readings

Webster, V. and Webster, A. (1997) *Raising Achievement in Hearing Impaired Pupils Supporting Teaching and Learning under the New Code of Practice*. Bristol: Avec Designs Ltd.
> This publication is a full and comprehensive description of many of the practical aspects of deaf education. The first section addresses, in particular, the Code of Practice and other relevant government legislation.

Gregory, S,. Knight, P., McCracken, W., Powers, S. and Watson, L. (1998) *Issues in Deaf Education*. London: Fulton Press.
> Chapter 5.3, 'Policy and Practice in the Education of Deaf Children and Young People', goes further into the implications for deaf children of much recent government legislation.

Chapter 10

The Deaf Child in School

Introduction

All parents hope that their children's experience of school is positive and successful. School experience plays a significant part in all children's lives which can influence and affect their growth into adulthood and the world of work. You are likely to be wondering to what extent your child's deafness might affect their school experience and overall achievement. While there are no straightforward answers to this, the aim of this chapter is to provide you with some general information about deaf children's school experiences.

The intention of this chapter is to consider what it is that deaf children bring to the learning situation which distinguishes them from their hearing peers. The implications of these identified differences are considered in terms of deaf children's potential for educational achievement and the role and expectations of services and schools for deaf children. Throughout this book we have stressed that deafness is not just a problem of auditory experience. The deprivation of sound is only one narrow view of deafness which can, in broader terms, be viewed as a cultural and linguistic issue as we have discussed in earlier chapters.

From this perspective we can focus on what deaf children can do on a par with their hearing peers, and more importantly, what they do differently from their hearing peers. Looking at deaf children's learning needs from this angle accepts that the difficulties that deaf children may experience in school are the result of an interaction between their learning needs and the educational setting rather than just a result of their deafness.

School places significant demands on all children as they meet with the succession of learning and social challenges from as early as four years old. Educational support for deaf children is not there to protect them from these challenges but to enable them to participate fully and to achieve their potential in all of these areas. Deaf children are entitled to the same learning opportunities as their hearing peers and teacher's expectations of them should be equally high. The expectations, the demands and the goals should therefore be the same but the nature of deafness makes the school experience for the deaf child different from that of the hearing child in several respects.

Deaf children come to school with very particular learning and social needs or characteristics which distinguish them from other groups of children with special educational needs. These characteristics obviously vary for individuals but we will talk in general terms for this section of the chapter. The areas which we will consider include:

- deaf children's areas of learning
  - general intelligence
  - reading and mathematics
  - general learning (cross-curricular) skills
- the school environment
  - the interaction between children and adults
  - language and communication choices

Deaf Children's General Intelligence

It is argued that deaf children think differently from the way hearing children do. This does not mean to say that they are not as intelligent or do not understand as well as hearing children, but just that their way of understanding and constructing the world is different. This is thought to be particularly true of children who are brought up using sign language. It is also thought that, in some areas of learning, deaf children may be more proficient than hearing children. This view of deaf children underlines a shift towards a much more positive view of deaf children as 'different' learners rather than as 'deviant' learners (deviant suggests they are doing something wrong rather than something different). This contrasts sharply with much of the earlier thinking about deaf children's general intelligence which focused on their weaknesses rather than on their strengths.

It is now stressed that the results of tests of intelligence on deaf children do indicate differences but not deviances. Marschark (1993: 129) explains that deaf children may have 'a different constellation of intellectual abilities'. He suggests a variety of reasons why deaf children may not perform as well as their hearing peers on conventional tests of intelligence. He stresses that these differences are not to do with an 'in child' problem but rather that they reflect deaf children's general lack of experience of learning through interaction with hearing peers and adults. He gives several examples of everyday direct and incidental learning experiences that deaf children may not encounter or may not be able to access fully such as:

- a parent's running commentary as they talk their child through a new experience or a change,
- opportunities to gain information and knowledge through incidental and indirect means such overhearing other child or adult conversations in the classroom, the commentary of the radio or television and
- knowledge gained from direct teaching in the classroom situation.

Marschark also suggests that deaf children may simply not be asked to solve problems by themselves or consider alternative solutions in school but this lack of experience should not be interpreted as an inability.

Types of intelligence tests

Tests of intelligence generally focus on the two main areas of verbal and non-verbal abilities. Verbal intelligence involves the use of language to solve problems or answer questions. Typical tests include matching vocabulary to pictures, giving opposites or recalling sequences of words or numbers. Non-verbal intelligence does not involve the use of language to solve problems or answer questions. Typical tests include remembering symbols, seeing patterns and sequences and visual discrimination.

It has been found that there is a remarkable similarity between deaf and hearing scores in intelligence tests. The most significant difference identified is that deaf children's verbal intelligence scores are generally lower than hearing children but deaf children's non-verbal intelligence scores are the same. It is also interesting to note that deaf children of deaf parents generally have much higher non-verbal intelligence scores than hearing children. These findings are extremely important when we think about the deaf child in school as it is clear that they do have the same potential to achieve success as hearing children in subjects or teaching approaches where non-verbal skills are emphasised.

Memory skills

Another significant difference between deaf and hearing children concerns the different development of memory. It has been found that deaf children's basic capacity for memory does not differ but that they use different ways to recall information. Deaf children's memory for visual information (remembering a map, a shape, a sequence of letters) is usually the same as their hearing peers. Deaf children's memory for information, which requires verbal or spoken rehearsal (counting sequences, alphabet), is usually less well developed than their hearing peers.

It is also suggested that deaf children who use sign language from birth can develop their non-verbal area of intelligence, that is their ability to organise space and remember spatial concepts (details of size, shape, movement, placement), to a better level than hearing children. This potential must be recognised as a learning strength for deaf children and channelled within the classroom.

If we are to take full advantage of the experience that a deaf child brings to school we need to be aware of the learning strengths which visual language can facilitate. Any differences that do exist for deaf children do not have to become barriers to learning in the educational setting. These differences place the responsibility on the teachers to ensure that deaf children develop and use these strengths to their advantage.

Literacy and Deaf Children

Developing reading and writing skills will probably be one of your most significant concerns as the parent of a deaf child. Deaf children's experience of learning to read and write is likely to be very different from that of most hearing children. It is therefore important to consider what deaf children bring to this particular learning situation. We live in a culture where speaking/listening and reading/writing are inextricably bound. From a very young age we all become aware of the possibility of storing or recording things, that we can see and hear, on paper. We learn to recognise that spoken and written language have very different purposes even before we are ourselves literate. We gain experience of what written language sounds like at an early age through story-telling and reading aloud. Although deaf children are also surrounded by this literacy culture, they may not experience it in the same way.

For children whose primary language is sign language the written word does not reflect the language that they use on a daily basis. Although they have a perfectly adequate way of communicating face-to-face, sign language currently has no written form. For these children, learning to read and write equates to learning a whole new language which is markedly different from sign language. In sign language meaning is expressed through the vision and gesture and several meanings can be conveyed at the same time. In written language meaning is expressed through a sequential organisation of words where only one meaning can be conveyed at once. Learning to read and write therefore requires a different understanding of language, how it is organised and how it expresses meaning. A more in-depth discussion of the processes involved in learning to read and approaches to developing deaf children's literacy takes place in the following chapter.

Mathematics and Deaf Children

Very little is known about deaf children's mathematical attainments compared to what is known about their reading and writing abilities. It has been found that even though deaf pupils, in general, are behind their hearing peers in their mathematical ability they are generally more successful with mathematics than they are with reading. Although this is a very positive finding we still need to know why mathematics presents some difficulties for deaf children. One argument is that mathematics has a specialist language and vocabulary which presents them with a number of linguistic problems (Gregory, 1998). For example:

- There is a particular specialist vocabulary in mathematics so children are meeting words the have never encountered before and indeed there may be no established sign for some of these words such as *remainder, area, estimate, fraction.*
- Everyday words from English are used in mathematics but with very specific meanings such as *difference, missing, similar, divide, regular, value, mean,* and this can be confusing for deaf children.
- Written instructions or task descriptions in mathematics have a very particular style which can be difficult to understand without a confident grasp of the written language, *e.g*
  'Draw lines to show how likely the following are'
  'give the reason why the total 7 never came up'.
- Mathematics uses symbols which are like a shorthand which allow a series of mathematical ideas to be linked together, deaf children may find it difficult to understand and use this shorthand which requires an understanding of the full English expression that it stands for.

Where deaf children do underachieve in mathematics, it is because of access (through English) to the mathematical concepts and a lack of understanding of the language of mathematics and not because of a lack of ability. We tend to think of mathematics as an area of the curriculum which does not require reading skills. We have shown that some very specific literacy skills are required which are likely to present difficulties for deaf children. Teachers of deaf children are now becoming more aware of this. Currently work is taking place looking into how sign language can be used to ensure deaf children's access to the concepts of mathematics avoiding the difficulties presented by the language of mathematics.

General Learning Skills

Independent learning

As well as developing reading, writing and number skills it is important that deaf children develop broader learning skills which prepare them for daily school life. One of the more general areas of learning deaf children need to establish is independence. This is not an uncommon difficulty faced by children with special educational needs and it is often reflected, in the case of young children, in later toilet training, self-feeding and safety behaviour. Although there is a limited amount of knowledge about the development of independence in school aged deaf children some explanations point to parental expectation and ways in which they interact with their deaf children. Difficulty in establishing independence can usually be explained by deaf children's lack of experience of learning through interaction with peers and adults.

For deaf children to take full advantage of school life they need to have practical independence skills and an independent approach to learning. These become essential as the children progress through their primary and secondary school lives. The following are examples in each of these areas for school-aged children.

Examples of practical independence skills

- arriving prepared for the classroom with the correct equipment and books, in the right place at the right time;
- organising own seating in the classroom so that watching and listening is optimised;
- using basic equipment safely without constant adult supervision;
- maintaining own hearing aids (settings, repair, replacement of batteries, ear moulds);
- developing and maintaining peer relationships;
- solving conflicts without adult intervention.

Examples of independent learning behaviour

- selecting an appropriate approach and the right materials for a given task;
- planning to complete the task in the time given;
- tackling a new task with little adult direction;
- overcoming new problems without asking for adult help;
- suggesting solutions for everyday problems; and
- seeking additional information independently (using dictionaries and reference books).

The establishment of independent learning behaviour is a priority for many teachers of deaf children and it is therefore important that parents and teachers work together. School can contribute a great deal to this area of development by:

- encouraging independent social and learning behaviour through example and positive feedback;
- providing experiences which deliberately develop the child's independence (not overprotecting them from unknown or challenging situations);
- having high expectations of the children;
- developing the pupils' confidence and self-esteem.

School does, however, only amount to a fraction of the child's time and so parents and teachers should work together to encourage these independence skills. As far as possible parents need to encourage their children to become independent in the home setting. Practical examples of this with school-aged children might include encouraging your child to:

- make their own decisions;
- make their own practical plans;
- prepare their own equipment;
- experiment and try out new experiences; and
- speak for themselves.

General knowledge

Another area of development which can significantly affect deaf children's learning is that of their acquisition of general knowledge. General knowledge can be described as factual information which is commonly shared by the general public. General knowledge is normally gained at home or in school through interaction, reading, radio and television, and through 'listening in' on the conversations of others.

Because general knowledge is largely gained through these experiences it is not surprising that deaf children do not always acquire levels of general knowledge equivalent with their hearing peers. Deaf children do not have access to information transmitted via the radio and their access to the television is restricted by the limited amount of sign language used and also by the level of reading needed to follow subtitles. As a result, deaf children may see things on television but not benefit from the accompanying commentary and explanation.

In the home, children normally gain general knowledge through the parent's running commentary on domestic, social and play activities as well as through explanation of special or unusual experiences. These opportunities may understandably be limited where the interaction between parent and child is not always easy.

In school a lack of general knowledge can create difficulties in terms of understanding the content of the different subject areas because a level of background knowledge is assumed. When an adult realises that there is a significant gap in the child's knowledge time has to be taken to bridge that gap which may affect the deaf child's progress through the subject area. There is also an important link between general knowledge and reading ability. It has been found that knowledge of vocabulary is crucial for reading comprehension. Vocabulary can be described as the labels for the ideas and concepts that already exist in the readers mind. Children with larger vocabularies are in general better readers and able to deal more confidently with new vocabulary that they meet in their reading. A child with a broader general knowledge has plentiful signs or words for things around them, that is to say they have a rich vocabulary.

These ideas point to a need for schools to systematically teach general knowledge. Greater awareness is also needed of where opportunities for gaining such knowledge may be missed and how this can be managed in school, for example, through the use of interpreters and deaf adults using sign language in the presence of deaf children. For this to be done successfully, consideration of the child's linguistic needs must be a priority. Providing the best language environment for each individual is discussed in detail later in this chapter.

At home parents can also help their children's development of general knowledge both through explanation and by providing, as far as possible, ongoing commentary on everyday events and activities. It does not matter which language is used for this. A deaf child's development of general knowledge through either sign language or English will greatly enhance their educational opportunities.

Critical thinking skills

Critical thinking involves a thoughtful, questioning and open-minded approach to learning. Some educators have argued strongly for developing deaf children's learning skills more broadly than just in subject areas, by concentrating on critical thinking skills. The rationale behind this argument is that the development of these skills offers deaf children additional learning opportunities and learning strengths. Critical thinking skills include the ability to recognise that there are often several different ways of approaching problems, no matter how simple or complex the problem may be. Critical thinking skills are relevant and useful for all learning situations (they are cross-curricular). They are valuable learning skills for all of the UK National Curriculum subject areas as these examples from the Programmes of Study for each of the core subjects demonstrate:

English: Speaking and Listening
Pupils should be encouraged to (. . .) indicate thoughtfulness about the matter under discussion (. . .) relate their contributions in a discussion to what has gone before, taking different views into account

Mathematics: Using and Applying Mathematics
Pupils should be taught to . . .

- develop different mathematical approaches and look for ways to overcome difficulties
- ask questions including what would happen if?. . . and why?

Science Experimental and Investigative Science
Pupils should be taught

- to recognise when a test or comparison is unfair
- to indicate whether the evidence collected supports any prediction made

Information technology
Pupils should be taught to

- interpret, analyse and check the plausibility of information held on IT systems . . .

As these examples demonstrate, critical thinking skills involve the ability to seek out and analyse given information, or evaluate a result or a finished product. They are, in fact, similar to research skills and can prepare learners for solving problems in all different aspects of life in school and beyond.

Critical thinking skills can build on what we already recognise as deaf children's learning strengths, such as their ability to use a visual–spatial language. For example, the visual properties of some signs actually reveal information about meaning. Because sign language can give extra information about meaning in this way, it may be possible to exploit this in the teaching situation. Where sign language is used to teach deaf children, its visual nature might help them to understand difficult concepts which will enhance their critical thinking skills.

Teacher-Pupil Interaction

The aspects of learning we have so far discussed have focused on the experiences and skills that deaf children bring with them to the learning situation. It is important to be aware, however, that some problems arise because of their actual experiences in the school setting. The interaction deaf children experience in school, both with adults and with peers, is a significant factor in terms of their academic success.

The way in which teachers communicate with deaf children was the subject of a very significant study in deaf education in the UK by Wood *et al.* (1986). We will explain the findings of this study because it has important implications for deaf children's learning. This study looked at the interaction between teachers of the deaf and their pupils in school. For children to develop language it is accepted that they need to have opportunities to use it freely and to receive meaningful feedback from those around them. However, it was found that certain types of teacher interaction actually inhibited the children's language use in the classroom.

The study focused on conversations which took place between pupils and teachers in oral/aural settings where all the teachers considered conversation to be a very significant part of their work in terms of developing the deaf children's spoken language skills. It was found that the ways in which the teachers controlled the conversation in the classroom directly influenced the children's language use and participation in the learning. The types of conversational control that the teachers used were grouped into the five categories listed in the table below. The categories are placed in order from most to least controlling and examples

Level of control	Examples
Enforced repetitions (requesting the child to repeat what they have said)	Say 'I have one at home'
Two-choice questions (giving the child a choice of two options to respond to a question)	Did you have a good time? Did you go with Jim or Pete?
Wh-type questions (asking open questions which do not require a prescribed answer)	What happened? Where did she go? Tell me about Sunday.
Personal contributions, comments, statements (commenting on the child's contribution without directing it)	That must have been awful. They call it a zoom lens. I love the lakes in Scotland.
Phatics (showing interest and encouraging further talk through emphatic comments)	Oh lovely! Super! I see. Hmm.

are given of the sorts of things that teacher might say in each category (adapted from Wood *et al.* (1986: 54).

This table shows that the lower levels of control allow the child to be more active in the conversation, that is, to be able to take control of the conversation themselves, contribute readily or introduce new topics. High levels of control, such as requests for repetitions or yes/no questions, force the children to respond using a set pattern of language rather than to take part in the conversation. The more control the teacher has over the conversation the more passive and uninvolved the child becomes. Another effect of the high level of teacher control in the conversation is that the children do not tend to address comments or questions to each other, whereas when the control is low, children converse and listen to each other.

This research provides a good illustration of the ways in which a learning problem can be exacerbated by factors within the school or classroom. The outcomes highlight the fact that some of the learning difficulties are not within-child problems but actually a result of the interaction between the learning needs of the children and their learning environment. This study made a considerable impact in the field of deaf education because of the value that teachers of deaf children normally place on conversation and oral interaction as a way of helping children acquire language. One of the positive outcomes of this research is that it has shown us successful ways of communicating with deaf children which support and encourage their spoken language development.

In the light of what we have learnt from this study, schools want to be sure that they meet the individual communication needs of deaf children. In the next section of the chapter we will look at ways in which decisions abut deaf children's communication needs are taken and present some examples of the different types of language programmes schools should be providing.

Meeting Deaf Children's Communication Needs in School

As a parent of a deaf child you will wish for your child to be educated in a setting where teachers and pupils interact meaningfully and where there is a shared language which allows your child to take a full part in school life. You are therefore looking for a school where each child's communication needs are taken into consideration. The ideal educational approach for all deaf children is one which recognises children's right to understand and to be understood whatever their preferred language. Such an approach will be based on the following principles.

All deaf children have an entitlement to:

- access the same curriculum as their hearing peers;
- communicate successfully and build positive relationships with deaf and hearing peers and adults;
- gain an age-appropriate level of competence in his or her preferred language (spoken language or sign language);
- gain a high level of skills in English as a second language (where appropriate);
- achieve his or her academic potential;
- develop a high level of self-esteem and sense of identity;
- become independent and resourceful learners in all areas of the curriculum; and
- develop independent social and life-skills.

What you look for in a school will depend on your child's learning and communication needs. Most importantly you will want to know how the school will support your child's language development. The educational needs of deaf children whose preferred language is BSL will differ from those whose preferred language is English. We now set out some guidelines which indicate what you might be looking for in either case. Effective educational support for deaf children will be organised to meet this full range of needs.

For a **child whose dominant language is sign language** the following provision should be made:

- BSL is used to teach all subject areas including English.
- The English teaching reflects the fact that the pupil is learning English as a second language (ESL), e.g. explicit teaching of grammar, using ESL curriculum frameworks, focus on the written form.
- The pupil's curriculum knowledge is assessed through BSL.
- There is access to a mixed group of BSL and English-dominant deaf and hearing children as well as links with the wider deaf community and heritage language community.
- BSL is considered to be a school subject with deaf studies so that pupils can be taught about their language and its origins and about deaf history, the deaf community and deaf organisations.
- The speaking and listening skills of each child are maximised and amplification of residual hearing is effectively managed (including cochlear implants) so that children are able to develop a range of strategies used for communicating with hearing people.

- Special assessments are used to monitor and assess the children's progress in BSL and English.

For a **child whose dominant language is English** the following provision should be made:

- English is used as to teach all subject areas.
- The development of the children's written and spoken language is assessed using the National Curriculum and other English language assessments.
- Manually Coded English (which incorporates the features of both sign language and English) is available as support for access to the full spoken form.
- Priority is given to maximising the child's speaking and listening skills through the use of residual hearing (including cochlear implants) and speech is seen as a primary language skill to be developed.
- Exposure to BSL is planned to enable the development of skills to socialise with deaf peers and adults and to foster mutual respect for English and BSL.
- There is access to a deaf peer group (sign language and English-dominant) and to hearing children (using English and heritage languages).
- The curriculum is assessed through English and manually coded English is used where it does not invalidate the assessment. (Adapted from Pickersgill & Gregory, 1998)

Language programmes should identify and address the following issues:

Individual language dominances

DANIEL needs a planned and sustained programme of work overseen and monitored by a teacher of the deaf for the development of age appropriate English speech and language skills.

ISSAN needs a planned and sustained programme of work administered and monitored by a deaf adult for the development of age appropriate BSL skills.

LEANNE needs a planned and sustained programme of work overseen and monitored by a teacher of the deaf for the development of a high level of skills in English as a second language with a particular emphasis on literacy skills and strategies for using spoken English.

> **The most appropriate means of access to the full curriculum**
>
> REBECCA needs access to the full curriculum and to the assessment activities through spoken English with appropriate visual and contextual support material in appropriate listening conditions.
>
> JAKE needs access to the full curriculum and to the assessment activities through BSL accompanied by focused support work on the English vocabulary and terminology of the different subject areas.

A school or service with only one fixed approach to communication is likely to have difficulty in meeting the full range of communication needs presented by the children and this raises some serious issues about children's entitlement to equality of opportunity and to a quality learning environment. In this chapter we have sought to focus on the individual child rather than on the communication debate.

Conclusion

It is often argued that deaf children's learning needs are no different from those of hearing children although a delay in the development of their overall intellectual development should be expected. This chapter has taken the view that deaf children do actually learn differently in some ways to hearing children and that they come to school with different abilities and that these different abilities should be recognised and harnessed. Expecting deaf children to develop and learn along the same lines as hearing children places them in a difficult situation where delay may be assumed as a matter of course. We would argue that learning support and intervention should pre-empt this as far as possible by taking account of deaf children's different learning styles and planning to target areas of difficulty and to build on their known and identified areas of strength.

Summary

This chapter has presented an overview of some of the central issues facing deaf children as learners in school. We have discussed the learning characteristics of deaf children and emphasised that they are the result of different early experiences and not a direct result of their deafness. We have also argued that the difficulties that some deaf children experience can be explained by the teaching style and the school environment where their learning needs are not fully considered or understood. Finally we have looked how a school can best be organised to meet the individual needs of all deaf children. We have given examples of this by contrasting

dren. Examples of objectives from individual children learning programmes have been used to illustrate practical approaches to ensuring
that all deaf children have the opportunity to succeed in the school
context.

Additional Reading

Gregory, S. (1998) Mathematics and deaf children. In S. Gregory, P. Knight, W.
McCracken, S. Powers and L. Watson (eds) *Issues in Deaf Education* (Chapter 3.1).
London: Fulton Press.
   This chapter provides an overview of the research into deaf children's achieve-
   ments in mathematics

Marschark, M. (1993) *Psychological Development of Deaf Children*. Oxford: Oxford
University Press.
   Chapter 4 presents a detailed discussion of deaf children social and personality
   development during the school years. Chapter 7 provides a thorough
   overview of the research into deaf children's intelligence and cognitive
   development.

Wood, D., Wood, H., Griffiths, A. and Howarth, I. (1986) *Teaching and Talking with
Deaf Children*. Chichester: Wiley.
   This book discusses important, and still relevant, research findings regarding
   deaf children's language, literacy and mathematical development in the school
   context.

Chapter 11
Learning to Read and Write

Introduction

One of the most significant milestones of your child's education is learning to read and write and all parents wish for their children to be successful in the development of these skills. Teachers of deaf children also know that literacy for a deaf child is fundamental to achieving equal participation and success in a hearing society and one of the central educational goals of deaf education is the attainment of, at least, age-appropriate literacy. There is extensive literature on the reading achievement of deaf children which shows that they generally struggle to become fluent and confident readers beyond 8–10 years of age. Despite this discouraging fact it is important to focus on deaf children's potential in this area as well as on their areas of difficulty. You will probably have many questions about reading and deafness and what can be done to help your child succeed in this area of learning. The aim of this chapter is therefore to guide you through some of these issues. We will explain the processes involved in learning to read and outline deaf children's strengths as well as the challenges they experience in becoming confident readers. Areas of strength that deaf children can develop and particular approaches to teaching literacy skills will also be discussed.

How we Learn to Read

The process of learning to read is itself very complex and so we shall start by explaining what is involved in this process and describe what successful readers do. Where we have had to use specific terminology this is explained fully in the text and also defined in the glossary.

What is reading?

Reading is the way in which we take meaning from print. It is not a passive activity but an interactive process between the reader and the text which requires the reader to be active and thinking. For a reading task to begin to be meaningful, the reader needs to have an understanding of the language system being used and some background knowledge of the topic of the text.

Models of reading

Our understanding of how children learn to read has been influenced by two contrasting theories which have attempted to explain what the reading process involves. These two theories are known as the **bottom-up theory** and the **top-down theory**. The bottom-up theory suggests that reading is a process of constructing the meaning using our knowledge of how the sounds (phonemes) match to the letters on the page (graphemes). This means that we gain our understanding by changing or decoding the letters on the page into the spoken words we know. This information gained from the print on the page leads to the discovery of meaning.

The bottom-up model of reading

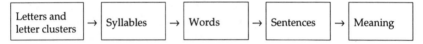

In contrast to this, the top-down theory argues that there is no such fixed progression from letters to words to meaning. This alternative view proposes that these visual and sound features are just one of the clues that the reader uses to make sense of what they read. This model proposes that a reader also approaches a text with expectations of what they are likely to find there and so is able to draw on their background knowledge and experience of language to make predictions about or guess the meaning of words and phrases. This model emphasises the reader's experience of the world and their understanding of the language as being more important than their ability to match the letters or patterns of letters with speech sounds.

The top-down model of reading

In our consideration of deaf children, including sign bilingual children, we will view the reading process as an interaction between the two models previously discussed, where the reader's top-down and bottom-up processes occur alongside each other. This **interactive model** recognises that the reader draws on information from three main sources in order to interpret the text. These sources of information are sometimes known as cueing systems and a fluent reader is able to draw on all of the following cueing systems to varying degrees, depending on their purpose for reading and their familiarity with the topic of the text.

The interactive model of reading

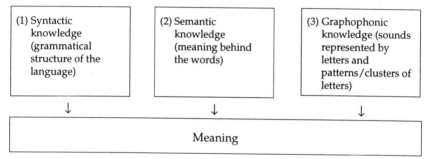

(1) Syntactic knowledge (grammatical structure of the language)	(2) Semantic knowledge (meaning behind the words)	(3) Graphophonic knowledge (sounds represented by letters and patterns/clusters of letters)
↓	↓	↓

Meaning

Using syntactic knowledge

Syntactic cues are cues that the reader gains from their knowledge of the grammatical structure of the language they are reading. The reader can predict what the word on the page is likely to be by using their previous knowledge of the language and its conventions.

Example

Lucy _____ the present.

From our knowledge of English we can predict that the missing word must be a verb such as *wanted, saw, wrapped,* or *opened*

Using semantic knowledge

Semantic cues help the reader to make sense of what they read using their experience of life and their world or cultural knowledge which is relevant to the particular text.

Example

On Lucy's birthday she _____ the present

Using our knowledge of what usually happens on birthdays in our culture we can predict that the missing word must be *'opened'*.

Using graphophonic knowledge

Graphophonic cues are cues that the reader gains from their knowledge of how the spoken language is represented through the written letters and patterns of letters, often referred to as spelling-to-sound rules. When a reader meets a new word in a text they might sound out the word according to the spelling-to-sound rules to help them work out the meaning of the word. They may make a guess using the initial letter sound or recognise a commonly occurring letter pattern such as 'ing'.

Example

Lucy o_____ the present.

Given the initial letter we can predict that the word is *'opened'* based on our knowledge of how the word sounds.

Successful readers are able to use all of these cues as they go through a continuous cycle of sampling, predicting and confirming their under-standing of a text. Difficulties arise for a reader if they are not able to use any of the cueing systems or if they are making insufficient use of any of these cueing systems. By analysing the reading process in this way we can identify where deaf children may experience particular difficulties.

How Deaf Children Learn to Read

For your deaf child to become a successful reader he or she needs to be able to use all of the three sources of information described previously. However, most deaf children do experience some difficulties in each area. We will explain some of these difficulties before moving on to look at ways in which we can support deaf children to become more successful readers at home and at school.

Deaf children's use of syntactic knowledge

To use syntactic cues the reader needs to have a knowledge of the language they are reading. This is normally developed through speaking and listening to the language. Because deaf children have limited access to the complete spoken form of English they may have difficulties in predicting meaning in text. This means that when your child comes to a word they do not know they may not have sufficient knowledge of how English fits together to make an informed guess about the type of word needed in that gap (e.g. a verb or a noun).

Deaf children also experience particular difficulties understanding the meaning of essential function words which sign up the reader's way through the text. Function words hold the text together because they link the ideas together. Function words include pronouns (*he, she, it, they, his*); connectives and conjunctions which link ideas (*and, after, before, unless, if*) and articles (*a, an, the*).

Another area of difficulty is following meaning across larger sections of text. Deaf children tend to focus on smaller units of meaning, such as individual words, because they cannot follow the connections between sentences. These connections are usually referred to as cohesive links. English creates cohesive links in several different ways and being able to carry an idea right through a text is dependent on the reader under-standing the cohesive link between sentences.

Two important ways in which English creates cohesive links are the use of reference words and the use of conjunctions. Reference words point to something in the text that has already be named or mentioned. They are words such as *he, she, it, here, there, the, this, those* and *that*. Deaf children may not recognise the link between the reference word and the object or person being referred to and this may impede their ability to follow the sense of what is written through a longer piece of connected text.

Example of Reference words

Every night now Tom slipped downstairs to the garden. At first *he* used to be afraid that *it* might not be there but *it* had never failed *him*.

Conjunctions link and organise ideas in a text. They are words like *and, but, because, so, unless, although, if, however, therefore*. Some conjunctions indicate a time sequence in a text and these might be *before, after, later* and *then*. Conjunctions help the reader to guess what might be coming next in a text and to predict the sort of meaning that will follow. The following example illustrates how these connections are made in written English and why they might be difficult to follow.

Example of Conjunctions

Once more, without hope, he raised his hand to the latch and pressed it. *As usual*, he could not move it *because* his fingers seemed to have no substance. *Then*, in anger, he pressed it *until* he felt that something had to happen. (adapted from *Tom's Midnight Garden* by Philippa Pearce)

Your deaf child may not understand the meanings that conjunctions bring to a text and this lack of language experience will hamper their ability to read with understanding and to pick out the main ideas within a text.

Your reaction to these areas of difficulty may be that you feel you need to provide more spoken language input for your child. However, several research projects have set out to investigate whether exposing deaf findings suggest that there are no grounds to advocate the exclusive use of either spoken or sign language but that exposure to both sign language and English, will have the most significant affect on your child's ability to tackle the syntactic component of reading.

Deaf children's use of semantic knowledge

Your child's knowledge of the world is linked to their knowledge of vocabulary. A vocabulary can be defined as the spoken, signed or written labels that a person has for things in their world. Our knowledge of the world is gained through information from spoken, written or signed language. The beginning deaf reader may come to the reading task with a limited knowledge of the world as a result of their limited early language experiences. They will therefore have fewer signs or words for the things in their world. If these readers are getting stuck because of lack of relevant vocabulary this reduces the speed at which they can process the text. As soon as reading speed is reduced the memory becomes overburdened and less effective as the reader tries to locate an unfamiliar word in their vocabulary store. As a result of this the reading process breaks down into a fragmented and frustrating experience.

The most significant finding of the research into deaf children's vocabulary is that deaf children seem to have gaps in their signed and oral vocabulary as well as in their written vocabulary. This suggests that vocabulary problems should not just be treated as English problems. The child's general linguistic development and world knowledge therefore needs to be expanded in both sign and spoken language.

The impact that this area of difficulty has on the child's experience of reading for meaning is very significant but there are ways in which this can be improved. Success in this area is self-perpetuating in that the bigger the reader's vocabulary becomes, the more able they are to deal with new vocabulary.

Deaf children are often more confident with the names of familiar objects around them (nouns) but struggle with less familiar abstract nouns of which they have less experience.

Examples of concrete familiar nouns		*Examples of abstract nouns*	
garden	tree	state	reason
wall	boy	idea	view
clock	friend	burden	grudge

One of the things that you can do as a parent is to ensure that you continue to expand your child's vocabulary in sign, speech and print beyond the concrete, practical and familiar and in this way, reduce the amount of times they get stuck on important meaning carrying words. This will increase their chances of experiencing reading as a connected and fluent experience.

Deaf children's use of graphophonic knowledge

When we introduced the role of graphophonic cues earlier in this chapter we talked about the relationship between sounds and spelling. You may wonder how your child will be able to make use of this sort of information. It would be easy to conclude that making use of these cues is not possible for many deaf children. It is true that some deaf readers may not be able to make use of sound–spelling information in the same way that hearing readers do and so they are not able to sound out new or unfamiliar words. Deaf children may not be clear about how the sounds of speech are represented by letters and clusters of letters and how punctuation relates to the intonation patterns of speech. However, current work in this area has highlighted the need to think in broader terms about phonological skills which include visual as well as spoken language skills. This is positive news for parents and teachers of deaf children.

Phonological awareness is an understanding of how letters and letter patterns relate to the pronunciation of the sounds of a language. There has recently been some research which has shown that phonological awareness does not necessarily just rely on hearing and speech ability. This means that deaf children can develop this understanding of how letters relate to speech sounds even though their speech ability and auditory experience may be limited. This phonological awareness can be developed through exposure to lip-reading, finger-spelling and writing although none of these is sufficient on its own to provide the breadth of language experience needed. This multi-channel approach allows deaf children to develop a visual picture of how letters and clusters of letters relate to speech sounds. In this way they can then use their visual knowledge of regular spelling patterns to make predictions and guesses about new words.

The development of your child's speech reading, articulation skills and use of their residual hearing will contribute significantly to their overall phonological awareness but it is important to appreciate that visual experience of a language (through lip-reading, finger-spelling and writing) can also help them to tackle unfamiliar text.

Deaf children of deaf parents

Deaf children of deaf parents tend to be more successful readers and writers than deaf children of hearing parents and there are several explanations for this. Some researchers suggest that deaf parents are able to better understand their children's communication needs because of their own experiences. Deaf children of deaf parents benefit from the early language experiences provided in the home setting. This situation is often harder for hearing parents to attain. You may be learning sign language at the same time as your child which means that it is more difficult for you to provide the linguistic experiences which draw the child's developing language forward.

Deaf parents are also more likely to have an understanding of where the child's difficulties with reading and writing lie, based on their own personal learning experiences. Because of this they are better placed to provide help and support exactly where it is needed. However, whether you are a deaf or a hearing parent your ability to use sign language with your child will lead to advantages in terms of their developing reading abilities.

Teaching Deaf Children to Read and Write

You will probably want to know how your child's teachers are teaching reading and writing to your child and what you can do to support this work in school. You will now appreciate that it is not always appropriate for schools to teach deaf children reading in exactly the same way as hearing children are taught. Hearing children are approaching reading with a different set of skills as the text they are working on reflects the spoken language they already know. Deaf children come to reading with a particularly unique language background and language learning situation as we have discussed in previous chapters. Research findings suggest that some deaf children's experience of learning to read and write is similar to that of hearing children for whom English is a second language. We should therefore respond to these similarities and use teaching approaches which capitalise on deaf children's different language learning skills.

More research is still needed into deaf children's experience of the reading and writing process and into how they develop specific skills so that these elements can be planned for in teaching programmes. For sign bilingual children, more account needs to be taken of their sign language skills and of ways in which these language skills can be channelled to enable them to become successful readers in their second language of English. We will now look at some of these developments in deaf education.

Developing children's metalinguistic awareness

One particular area which needs to be further developed is our understanding of deaf children's metalinguistic awareness. Metalinguistic awareness requires a more abstract knowledge and understanding of language which involves the ability to think and talk about language, to recognise characteristics of a language and to see how language is structured. One example of this would be where your child begins to ask you why you have used a certain word or sign. If you are learning sign language or another second language you will probably making comparisons between English and the language you are learning and this demonstrates a level of metalinguistic awareness. For sign bilingual deaf children with limited access to the spoken form of the language they are learning, the development of metalinguistic understanding may provide an alternative means of tackling the written form of English.

Metalinguistic skills can only be part of teaching reading and writing if sign language plays a significant role in the teaching process. Professionals working in bilingual programmes are now starting to explore ways of teaching literacy in this way. Some effective examples of where this approach has been adopted with sign bilingual children are to be found in Sweden and Denmark where bilingual education for deaf children is widely accepted. In both countries, Swedish (SSL) and Danish Sign Language (DSL) respectively are used as the language of the classroom and are also taught as curriculum subjects in their own right.

Teaching reading and writing in Scandinavia

Bilingual approaches to teaching in Sweden and Denmark share these two key principles:

- Emphasis is placed on the learner's continued development of knowledge and skills in sign language at pre-school level.
- Learners are taught to analyse sign language and to use it to discuss features of the written second language and to be able to compare and contrast sign language with the written language.

Reviews of bilingual education in Denmark and Sweden suggest that deaf students in bilingual classes demonstrate reading levels comparable to those of their hearing peers. This is why the approaches used there are of interest to parents and teachers elsewhere. One reported teaching approach from Sweden incorporates the use of a specially designed children's book and parallel SSL video tapes which centre on a deaf child and his family. Emphasis is placed on discussion and comparisons between the grammar of the two languages rather than on word-for-word reading of the written Swedish. In this way children are allowed to discover for themselves the contrasting and similar ways in which meaning can be communicated in both languages. The use of signing and talking at the same time is avoided as teachers say that it is easier to talk about two languages when they are kept clearly separate.

In Denmark approaches also include this comparison and some translation work but spoken Danish is seen as being as integral to the development of literacy skills. The use of manually coded Danish for word-for-word reading aloud is accepted as a transitional phase in learning to read. At the Copenhagen School for the Deaf the children work in groups to translate the DSL story into a written Danish version and then practice reading the written version aloud, without sign support, following the teacher's indications of rhythm and phrasing.

Teaching reading and writing in the UK

Currently in the UK, more and more schools and services are describing their approach as bilingual. In the current sign bilingual educational setting the prerequisites for teaching literacy share the principles outlined in the Swedish and Danish models:

- British Sign Language (BSL) and spoken and written English are both taught as curriculum subjects.
- A basis of skills in BSL is recognised as central to the successful learning of English literacy.
- BSL is used to teach English.
- The children's language awareness skills established in BSL are expected to be transferable to their English literacy learning.
- Manually Coded English (MCE) is for clearly defined teaching purposes such as supporting the learner's exposure to the spoken form of English.

This does not mean that your deaf child will not be following the same curriculum as his or her hearing peers. Sign bilingual children do work towards the same National Curriculum literacy goals as their hearing peers although English literacy is likely to be taught as a second language where the skills focus, the teaching approaches and the materials are more appropriate for their particular learning needs. Across the small number of schools and services working in this way there are some common approaches and teaching materials which are currently being developed.

Reading for meaning

The use of DARTs (Directed Activities Related to Text) has been found to be a successful teaching strategy in sign bilingual approaches. DARTs is an activity-based approach aimed at enabling children with limited reading skills to read for meaning. DARTs help pupils to find information in the text by giving them structured analysis and reconstruction tasks to do. These tasks actively involve them in the text and encourage them to see reading as a means of learning across the curriculum and not as a discrete activity. DARTs have been popular with teachers working with sign bilingual children because they can be designed for individuals, they encourage group work and discussion and they give deaf children useful ways of extracting meaning from text.

Purposeful writing

Dialogue journals are also a common feature of sign bilingual approaches. A dialogue journal is a shared journal in which adult and learner communicate in writing on any topic. The communication is natural, purposeful and individual and the pupils are motivated to contribute and keep this contact going. The adult responds to but does not correct the pupil's English. This makes the communication some-what special and personal and encourages pupils to attempt writing things in English that they would not otherwise risk. The adult does have the opportunity to model the correct written English for the pupil in their response and so can extend their reading and writing skills in this way. The children are highly motivated to keep a journal, especially with a deaf adult, and so they provide an ideal opportunity to give deaf children the experience of real communication through the written form of English.

A focus on grammar

Professionals involved in teaching literacy to sign bilingual deaf children have drawn teaching ideas and curriculum materials from the fields of foreign and second language teaching. One of the particular principles which has been adopted is the importance of making children aware of patterns in language and making the grammar rules of language more accessible to them. Alongside a more formal approach to grammar teaching some of the more communicative aspects of foreign and second language teaching have been adapted for sign bilingual settings. These include the importance of learning language in real-life situations; an emphasis on top-down skills such as the ability to use contextual cues and prior experiences to interpret text and infer meaning; and the importance of metalinguistic skills such as the ability to talk about, compare and contrast languages.

Formal approaches to language teaching focus on	Communicative approaches to language teaching focus on
• how the language is structured • how the language is used • conscious learning and practice	• the message not the structure • the purpose of the communication • real communication needs of the learner

Hearing children's development of reading and writing is based on their skills in spoken language. Many deaf children may come to literacy with developing rather than age-appropriate sign language skills and only basic skills in their second language of English. Even deaf children who have grown up in a sign language environment and already have age-appropriate sign language skills when they first begin to learn English are likely to experience some difficulties. It is for these reasons that innovative approaches to the teaching of reading and writing which capitalise on the role of sign language in the teaching and learning process are being developed in bilingual approaches in the UK and beyond.

The role of spoken language

In the teaching approaches that are developing for sign bilingual children, the role of spoken language is seen as supporting the literacy process but not as a prerequisite for the development of reading and writing skills. Wherever possible learners are taught to draw on their spoken language skills to support the development of their literacy skills. It is also accepted that for some sign bilingual children the spoken language cannot provide a bridge to the written form. For these children emphasis is placed on the development of more analytical language learning strategies

Ways Forward

There is no one accepted method for teaching reading to all deaf children but there are indications that certain factors can help towards reading success. Now that you have more information about the reading process and deaf children's experience of this that you can see how parents can play a role in this. There follows some suggestions about ways in which you can support your child's literacy development. It is important that you consider these as tips to make your reading or book-sharing activities more enjoyable and not feel that you have to take on the role of teacher in the home context. You might find it useful to use one or two of these strategies from time to time when you feel it is appropriate. We do emphasise that this is not a list of what parents should do every time they share a book with their child but a list of ideas, some of which you might find useful. Many of the suggestions are things that parents do naturally when reading with their young children and the emphasis should remain on the enjoyment of the activity.

Extending your child's vocabulary and world knowledge

- Discuss what they know about the topic of the book before you begin reading.
- Try to introduce new vocabulary and language structures as you talk.

Developing your child's understanding of the structures of English

- Draw your child's attention to grammatical features in the text such as word endings or punctuation.
- Show your child how a text holds together, through the use of connecting words.

Encourage pupils to read reflectively, for meaning

- Ask your child questions about the book before they start to read to help their reading for meaning.
- Give your child the opportunity to read silently and to explain what they have read to you.
- Encourage your child to skim a page for the general gist or look for specific information.

Develop your child's broader phonological skills.

- Ensure that your child has some supported exposure to the spoken form of English.
- Encourage your child to recognise patterns of rhythm and rhyme in songs, nursery rhymes and poems.

Develop your child's awareness of language

- Draw your child's attention to the similarities and differences between sign language and English (for example how one sign might equate to two or more words).

- Encourage your child to talk about the areas of literacy learning they find easy or difficult.

The emphasis placed on the structural and grammatical features of English in the National Literacy Project (NLP) in the UK is highly relevant for deaf children who will benefit from the more explicit teaching and explanation of language. What is important to consider in the light of this Government strategy is how to ensure that deaf children have full access to high quality and intense literacy instruction and how sign language can best be used to support this process.

Conclusion

We hope that this chapter will support you in becoming more involved in your child's literacy development and enable you to ask the questions you need to of teachers and other professionals. The central message of this chapter is that it is important not to consider deaf pupils' literacy achievements solely in the context of their hearing peers. We must recognise that they are a unique group of language learners. Rather than focusing on what they cannot do we must continue to explore what different strategies they have as learners so that teaching approaches can be developed which match their specific needs. Above all, literacy should become an enjoyable and fun part of the deaf child's life both at home and at school. Sitting down with your child and reading or signing a book is the best way to support their reading development. Parents do not need to train their children but simply to share the pleasures of books and read with them as a child's personal motivation for learning to read is the most powerful attribute that they can bring to the learning context.

Summary

This chapter has outlined the processes involved in learning to read and write and discussed areas of learning which deaf children find difficult. We have stressed that despite the identified areas of difficulty, deaf children do bring different skills to the reading process which need to be recognised and harnessed. We have looked at actual teaching approaches and particularly at ways in which sign language can be used to support deaf children's literacy development. Approaches in the UK and beyond have been described. Finally we have made some suggestions of ways in which parents can support their deaf child's reading development.

Additional Reading

Marschark. M. (1993) _Psychological Development of Deaf Children_. Oxford: Oxford University Press.
   Chapter 11 discusses deaf children's reading and writing abilities.

Lewis, S. (1998) Reading and writing within an oral/aural approach. In S. Gregory, P. Knight, W. McCracken, S. Powers and L. Watson (eds) _Issues in Deaf Education_ (Chapter 3.1). London: Fulton Press.

Swanwick, R. (1998) The teaching and learning of literacy within a sign bilingual approach. In S. Gregory, P. Knight, W. McCracken, S. Powers and L. Watson (eds) _Issues in Deaf Education_ (Chapter 3.2). London: Fulton Press.
   The two chapters above outline the theoretical and practical implications of literacy development and describe current some current teaching strategies within two contrasting communication approaches.

Conclusion

This book has presented a perspective on deafness which, it is hoped, will positively inform and support all those involved in raising and educating deaf children.

Parents

Bringing up children is never easy and deaf children are no exception. There are emotional and practical pressures to be acknowledged and responded to. Usually these pressures reduce with support from both other families with similar experiences and the fullest possible information about all aspects of deafness. The appreciation that there are similarities as well as differences between deaf and hearing children means that deaf children can viewed as individuals with their own identity. This has been reflected in the central theme of this book; that is supporting deaf children in relation to this identity. This means that issues of appropriate language availability and teaching strategies remain of paramount importance. That these issues are now being addressed both in support to families and in education is a reflection of changing attitudes and a broader perspective on deafness.

Education

In education, a gradual shift is beginning towards this broader perspective, although much work remains to be done to precipitate and secure this change. It is important, however, to recognise and celebrate the achievements so far. To conclude the educational themes discussed in this book we will review what has been achieved and point to future priorities.

Changing Perspectives

The constraints that deafness places on language development and educational achievement present deaf children with particular learning needs in the areas of language and literacy which have to be addressed within a special educational needs framework. This perspective has dominated deaf education which has, up until recently, focused on the impairment of deafness and the subsequent barriers to learning. However, because many deaf children approach the educational context learning the two languages of sign language and English, some of their learning needs can also be considered within the context of bilingual education. This perspective has enabled educators to focus on the linguistic rather than the medical aspects of deafness and hence to plan constructively for the use of two languages in deaf children's education. This positive recognition of the bilingual potential of deaf children and the 'grass-roots' work undertaken to develop and implement appropriate educational programmes has shaped a model of sign bilingual education.

Towards a Model of Sign Bilingual Education

The recently accepted use of the term 'sign bilingual' in England signifies at once the similarities and differences between deaf and hearing bilinguals. The use of the term 'bilingual' to describe deaf children suggests that deaf people do belong to a the larger community of bilingual (hearing and deaf) people but to use 'bilingual' as the sole descriptor would be to place deaf bilingual people within a group where they do not comfortably sit. The use of the term 'sign bilingual' makes the distinction needed between bilingualism involving two spoken and written languages and sign bilingualism which involves two languages but three modalities (signed, spoken and written). The use of the term sign bilingual recognises that either sign language or English may be a child's preferred language. It is also recognised that the use of a mixed code such as a form of manually coded English is a normal component of deaf children's linguistic repertoire. This move towards a more clearly defined educational model, which accepts individual language differences, is a significant milestone. This development signals increasing confidence in the sign bilingual educational model as an appropriate approach for all deaf children.

Sign Bilingual Education: The Current Picture

Two fundamental developments in bilingual and deaf education provided the impetus for the establishment of sign bilingual education for deaf children. These are the evidence of the positive aspects of bilingualism in general which began to emerge in the early 1970s and the recognition of BSL as a naturally evolved and fully fledged language.

Sign bilingual education for deaf children has been established in parts of the UK only since the late 1980s and in practical terms continues to be reappraised, improved and more clearly defined. It is recognised that our understanding of sign bilingualism is rapidly developing although much of our understanding is based on the bilingual language development of hearing children learning two spoken languages. At an international level, Scandinavia and North America are making significant contributions to this developing area in the areas of both practice and research although still little information on educational outcomes is available.

In Sweden and Denmark sign language is part of the curriculum for all deaf students and both countries offer intensive training in sign language for parents and teachers. Linguistic researchers into sign language and deaf and parental organisations have combined forces in both countries to bring about change in the education system for deaf children. Two significant landmark events in the 1980s were that first in 1983, the Swedish Government officially recognised Swedish Sign language as the native language of deaf people in Sweden. Secondly, in 1987 moves were made in Denmark at government level to incorporate the teaching of Danish Sign Language in all schools for deaf children and this finally became an educational entitlement in 1992. The development of sign bilingual education has not been tackled so systematically with government support elsewhere. Despite the lack of a shared international commitment to a sign bilingual philosophy developments are constantly taking place at the 'grass-roots' level. These can be discussed in the areas of sign language, spoken language and literacy development.

Sign Language Development Within a Sign Bilingual Approach

Within the current model of sign bilingual education, it is not assumed that deaf children will simply catch sign language skills and develop them to an age-appropriate level by working with deaf adults from pre-school upwards. It has been identified that deaf children need exposure to the adult form of sign language being used in natural communicative situations. It has therefore become increasingly standard to have sign language and deaf studies teaching on the timetable and to ensure that deaf children have exposure to sign language being used fluently between adults on a daily basis. Up until now there has been no mechanism for measuring the development of children's sign language skills as there has been no established curriculum and no recognised milestones of development. However, an assessment is currently being developed in the UK which will indicate norms for receptive and productive BSL grammar for children aged between four and eleven years. This will enable baseline measures to be taken and for progress in BSL development to be monitored.

Literacy Development Within a Sign Bilingual Approach

It is argued that deaf pupils' developing sign language skills should be recognised as an area of strength with regard to literacy learning and that these skills provide the main route into literacy development. This implies a structured approach to literacy learning which emphasises the direct teaching of literacy skills. Deaf children are not likely to be able to fully experience enough spoken language input to be able to develop an internal representation of how that language works and therefore some direct teaching and learning of the structure of that language must take place. It is argued that if deaf children engage in formal language learning activities they will develop a higher level of metalinguistic skills, that is the ability to reflect on and talk about one's own language learning experiences. It is thought that this ability to stand back and reflect on language will enable deaf pupils to benefit from the formal teaching of literacy skills. This is another developing area where experimental action research is currently taking place, which, it is anticipated, will provide alternative routes to literacy development for deaf children.

The Place of Spoken Language Within a Sign Bilingual Approach

It is a misconception to think that there is no place for speech development within a sign bilingual approach. On the contrary, spoken language has a very considered role within this approach. Within a sign bilingual approach the success of an individual's education is not measured only in terms of their spoken language development. Pupils are given maximum opportunity to develop their spoken language skills as part of their whole education. Many children are able to benefit from this but it is recognised that for some children written language may be more accessible than spoken language. This differs from an oral/aural frame-work where the development of spoken language skills are considered to be of primary importance and a prerequisite for the development of literacy skills.

Another significant difference is that literacy is seen as a support for spoken language development. It appreciated that the majority of speech sounds are not perceptible through speech reading and that text provides pupils with the phonological, lexical and syntactical information needed to make sense of speech reading. Various strategies are being explored within the sign bilingual approach to clarify and support the spoken form in order to give pupils fuller access to natural spoken language. Where sign language is used for instruction and explanation in the development of deaf children's spoken language skills deaf children's potential in this area can be properly tapped within a supportive learning context. As this area of practice continues to develop the goals of oral/aural education can be addressed within the sign bilingual model.

Outcomes of Sign Bilingual Education

A current focus of sign bilingual education is the need for information about deaf children's achievements within this approach. Up until now deaf children's achievements have only been recognised from an oral/ aural perspective because sign bilingual educational programmes are few in number and only relatively recent. A few research projects are to be found which lead to concrete findings about achievements or learning styles of sign bilingual deaf children but work remains to be done on the development of assessment procedures which reflect sign bilingual children's different abilities.

Although these priorities sound academic it is parents and teachers of deaf children who can make the most significant contribution to our developing understanding. Teachers have at their fingertips evidence of individual children's learning processes and achievements. The much needed collation of comprehensive records of deaf pupils' progress and achievements in sign bilingual settings relies on this information. Parents have different insights into their children's progress and development and this is also valuable information. Parents are also in a position to ask questions and be critical of the educational support available.

It is the parents and teachers who so far have been the agents of change in deaf education through asking the difficult questions in the wider educational forum. Parents and teachers of deaf children must continue to be agents of change although this is not an easy path to travel. This requires a recognition of the gaps in our knowledge about sign bilingualism along with a commitment to reviewing, and improving established practice. It is because of this commitment that so much has already been achieved.

Appendix

Otitis Media with Effusion (Glue Ear)

Otitis media with effusion is better known as 'glue ear' and is a very common condition in children, especially under the age of five. A study by Brooks (1974) found the incidence of glue ear in children to be as follows.

Age (years)	Percentage of children experiencing at least one incidence of glue ear
Under 4	35
5	20
6	12
7	8
8	6
9	3
over 9	2.5

As you can see, glue ear is very common in small children, but it is also something they grow out of. However, from an educational point of view, the early years are formative and, consequently, education may suffer if glue ear is allowed to go undetected or untreated. The important point to remember about glue ear is that it is a fluctuating loss. The child's hearing acuity can vary from month to month, week to week and even day to day. It is for this reason that glue ear is often difficult to pinpoint and why sometimes children are labelled 'difficult' because they appear to hear 'when they want to'.

What is Glue Ear?

As we discovered earlier, the middle ear plays a vital part in the transmission process of hearing. Its function is to transmit and amplify sound waves on their way to the cochlea. For the middle ear to function properly the ear drum and ossicle bones must be free to vibrate at atmospheric pressure. Atmospheric pressure is maintained by the opening and closing of the eustachian tube to allow a fresh supply of air into the middle ear. Glue ear is the result of a eustachian tube which has become blocked. This can be caused by enlarged tonsils or adenoids, which are positioned very close to the opening of the eustachian tube at the back of the throat. It can also be caused by a slight infection which causes the eustachian tube to swell and consequently become blocked. The fact that in such young children the eustachian tube is very small exacerbates the problem, as does the fact that the eustachian tube has a slightly more horizontal 'gradient' in small children than in adults. What ever the cause, the effect is a blockage of the eustachian tube and consequently the air in the middle ear cannot be replaced.

The oxygen in the air in the middle ear is constantly being absorbed by the surrounding membrane. Because this air cannot be replaced negative pressure begins to build up. This starts to suck the ear drum inwards, making it less flexible and less able to transmit sound waves effectively. Then negative pressure also tends to suck in opening of the eustachian compounding the original problem. As negative pressure continues to build up, and the eustachian tube remains blocked. Fluid, secreted by the membrane of the middle ear, starts to fill the middle ear cavity. This has the effect of reducing the mobility of the ossicles and their ability to transmit and amplify sound waves. As time goes by, the fluid becomes thicker and more viscous until it eventually 'anchors' both the ear drum and the ossicles causing a significant conductive hearing loss.

In some instances the build-up of pressure behind the ear drum can become so great that the ear drum ruptures under the pressure. This will have the effect of releasing the fluid, and if the cause of the blocked eustachian tube has cleared up the problem will resolve itself without medical intervention. The ear drum will repair itself in a matter of days and hearing will return to normal.

This rupturing of the ear drum is not desirable, however, and for this reason, other methods are often used to treat glue ear.

Sometimes the doctor will prescribe antibiotics to clear up the infection or decongestants to dry the fluid. If these do not work then the child can be referred to the ENT clinic for further investigation. The ENT surgeon might decide to remove the tonsils and adenoids to prevent the problem re-occurring. The surgeon may also decide to insert a **grommet**.

A **grommet** is a tiny plastic tube a little bit like a cotton reel. The grommet is inserted into the ear drum whilst the child is under general anaesthetic. Before inserting the grommet, the doctor will suck out the fluid that has built up in the middle ear by way of a tiny cut in the ear drum. This known as a **myringotomy.** Having sucked out the fluid, the grommet is then inserted. The function of the grommet is to allow air into the middle ear through the hole in its centre until the Eustachian tube is fully functional again.

Some children are fitted with **T tubes**. These have exactly the same function as grommets but are shaped like a T instead of like a cotton reel. Because of their shape they are less likely to fall out before their remedial purpose has been achieved.

Some grommet operations are very successful and the problem of glue ear does not recur. However, some children need a number of grommets inserted before the process is successful and for some children, the problem remains ongoing. On the whole doctors do not carry out more than four grommet operations on the same ear, as this causes a build-up of scarring tissue which can result in permanent loss of flexibility to the ear drum. Grommets very rarely need to be removed, as they tend to work their way out naturally over time. Some work their way out too quickly before their remedial purpose has been achieved. When this happens, the doctor may decide on a further grommet insertion.

As mentioned earlier, glue ear is a very common problem in very young children but they do grow out of it by the age of eight or nine. Consequently, there is s some professional controversy about treatment using grommets. Some doctors believe in inserting grommets as soon as the problem occurs, others prefer to wait until it is known that the problem is chronic, others are against grommet operations per se and prefer nature to take its course, waiting until children grow out of it. The type of treatment children can expect, therefore, depends very much upon the area in which they live and the practice of the ENT surgeon. Because glue ear is such common problem in children, there is often discussion of the advantages and disadvantages of grommets in the press. Keep an eye out for current thinking on grommet operations in your daily paper.

Acute and Chronic Otitis Media

Otitis media simply means an ear infection. For the duration of the infection, pus builds up behind the ear drum and can cause severe earache due to increased pressure. When the ear is full of infected pus, the ossicles and ear drum will not operate efficiently causing a conductive loss. Often the infection results in the ear drum bursting. When this happens the earache is relieved due to the release of the pressure. Acute otitis media is a 'one off' infection and the ear drum heals in time, without leaving any lasting damage.

Some children suffer from chronic otitis media which brings a continuing, ongoing pattern of ear infection as well as the discomfort and difficulties experienced at the time. Sometimes long-term hearing damage occurs through a permanent perforation or distruction of the ossicle bones by infection. It is possible to repair the ear drum and replace the ossicles, but usually ENT surgeons will wait until the child reaches about 16 or 17 before carrying out this sort of operation. In the meantime, the child will have to contend with a significant hearing loss and may well need a hearing aid.

The above information has been reproduced with the permission of K. Andrews and N. Roberts, the authors of *Helping the Hearing-impaired Child in Your Class* (Oxford: Oxford Brookes University Press, 1994).

Useful Addresses

Information about Deaf Societies

National Deaf Children's Society (NDCS)
15, Dufferin Street, London EC1Y 8PD, UK
Tel: 0171 2500123 voice and text
Fax: 0171 2515020

British Deaf Assocation (BDA)
1–3 Worship Street, Moorgate, London EC2A 2AB, UK
Tel: 0171 5883250
Text: 0171 588 352
Fax: 0171 5883527

Royal National Institute for the Deaf (RNID)
19–23 Featherstone Street, London EC1 8SL
Tel: 0171 296 8000
Text: 0171 296 8001
Fax: 0171 296 8199

Information about Language Issues

Deaf Education Through Listening and Talking (DELTA)
PO Box 20, Haverhill, Suffolk CB9 7BD, UK
Tel: 01440 783 689 (voice and fax)

Language and Sign as an Educational Resource (LASER)
c/o Miranda Pickersgill, Blenheim Center, Crowther Place, Leeds
LS6 2ST, UK
Tel: 0113 2429111

Information about Learning Sign Language

Council for the Advancement of Communication with Deaf People (CACDP) Pelaw House, School of Education, University of Durham, Durham DH1 1TA, UK

Text Answering Machine: 0191 3747864
Fax: 0191 374 3605

Information about Schools and Education

NDCS DIRECTORY
see NDCS

Information about Deaf, Blind and Rubella Children

National Deaf, Blind and Rubella Association (SENSE)
11–13 Clifton Terrace, London N4 3SR
Tel: 0171 272 7774
Text: 0171 272 9648
Fax: 0171 272 6012

Information about Cochlear Implants

Northern Region (Support Group)
Hilary French, 1, Wearside Drive, The Sands, Durham City, Co. Durham DH1 1LE, UK
Tel: 0191 386 1112

Southern Region (Support Group)
Mrs T. Kemp, 4 Ranelagh Avenue, Barnes, London SW13 0BY, UK
Tel: 0181 876 8605

United States of America

Alexander Graham Bell Association for the Deaf
3417, Volta Place, NW, Washington DC 20007, USA
Tel: 202 337 5220

American Society for Deaf Children
2848 Arden Way, Suite 210, Sacramento, California, CA 95825–1373, USA
Tel: 916482 0120 (voice and text)
1.800 942 asdc (voice and text)
Fax: 916 482 0121

John Tracey Clinic
806 West Adams Boulevard, Los Angeles, California, CA 90007, USA
Tel: (213) 7485481
Text: (213) 747 2924
Fax: (213) 749 1651

National Association of the Deaf
814 Thayer Avenue, Silver Spring, Maryland, MD 20910-4500, USA
Tel: 301 587 1788
Text: 301 587 1789
Fax: 301 587 1791

References

Andrews, E. and Roberts, N. (1994) *Helping the Hearing Impaired Child in your Class*. Oxford: Oxford Brookes University Press.

Baker, C. (1996) *Foundations of Bilingual Education and Bilingualism*. Clevedon: Multilingual Matters.

Bloomfield, L. (1933) *Language*. New York: Holt.

Bouvet, D. (1990) *The Path to Language*. Clevedon: Multilingual Matters.

Brennan, M. (1976) Can deaf children acquire language? *Supplement to the British Deaf News* (February).

Brennan, M. and Brien, D. (1995) Defining the bi in bilingualism. In H. Bos and T. Schermer (eds) *Sign Language Research 1994* (pp. 257–72). Hamburg: Signum Press.

Department of Health (1989) *The Children Act*. London: HMSO.

DES (1978) *Special Educational Needs (Warnock Report)*. London: HMSO.

DES (1981) *Education Act*. London: HMSO.

DES (1988) *Education Reform Act*. London: HMSO.

DfEE (1993) *Education Act*. London: HMSO.

DfEE (1997) *Excellence for all Children Meeting Special Educational Needs*. London: HMSO.

Erting, C. (1992) *Partnership for Change: Creating New Possible Worlds for Deaf Children and Their Families* Washington, DC: Gallaudet University Press.

Erting, C (1993) *Deafness, Communication and Social Identity*. Burtonsville, MD: Linstok.

Fletcher, L. (1987) *Language for Ben*. London: Souvenir Press.

Freeman, R., Carbin, C. and Boese, R. (1981) *Can't Your Child Hear?* London: Croom Helm.

Gregory, S. (1998) Mathematics and deaf children. In S. Gregory, P. Knight, W. McCracken, S. Powers and L. Watson (eds) (1998) *Issues in Deaf Education*. London: Fulton Press.

Gregory, S., Knight, P., McCracken, W., Powers, S. and Watson, L. (eds) (1998) *Issues in Deaf Education*. London: Fulton Press.

Gregory, S., Smith, S. and Wells, A. (1997) Language and identity in sign bilingual deaf children. *Deafness and Education* (BATOD) 21(3), 31–8.

Grosjean, F. (1992) The bilingual and the bicultural person in the hearing and in the deaf world. *Sign Language Studies* 77, 307–20.

Kannapell, B. (1993) *Language Choice – Identity Choice*. Burtonsville, MD: Linstok Press.

Knight, P. (1998) Disability and deafness. In S. Gregory, P. Knight, W. McCracken, S. Powers and L. Watson (eds) *Issues in Deaf Education*. London: Fulton Press.

Ladd, P. (1991). Making plans for Nigel. In G. Taylor and J. Bishop (eds) *Being Deaf: The Experience of Deafness*. Milton Keynes: The Open University Press.

Lane, H., Hoffmeister, R. and Bahan, B. (1996) *A Journey into the DEAF-WORLD*. San Diego, CA: DawnSign Press.

LASER (1995) *Cochlear Implantation and Bilingualism*. Leeds: LASER.

Lewis S. (1998) Reading and writing within an oral/aural approach. In S. Gregory, P. Knight, W. McCracken, S. Powers and L. Watson (eds) *Issues in Deaf Education*. London: Fulton Press.

Marschark, M. (1993) *Psychological Development of Deaf Children*. Oxford: Oxford University Press.

Marschark, M. (1997) *Raising and Educating a Deaf Child*. Oxford: Oxford University Press.

McCormick, B., Archbold, S. and Sheppard, S. (1995) *Cochlear Implants for Young Children*. London: Whurr.

Mahshie, S.N. (1995) *Educating Deaf Children Bilingually*. Washington, DC: Gallaudet University Press.

McCracken, W. and Sutherland, H. (1991) *Deaf-Ability —Not Disability*. Clevedon: Multilingual Matters.

Meadows-Orlans, K. (1990) Research developmental aspects of deafness. In D. Moores and K. Meadows-Orlans (eds) *Educational and Developmental Aspects of Deafness*. Washington, DC: Gallaudet University Press.

Moores, D. F. (1996) *Educating the Deaf: Psychology, Principles and Practice*. Boston, MA: Houghton Mifflin.

Oestreicher, J. P. (1974) The early teaching of modern language, education and culture. *Review of the Council for Cultural Cooperation of the Council of Europe* 24, 9–16.

Padden, C. (1991) The deaf community and the culture of deaf people. In S. Gregory and G. Hartley (eds) *Constructing Deafness*. Milton Keynes: The Open University Press, Pinter Publishers Ltd.

Padden, C. (1994) The bicultural. *Signpost* (Winter), pp. 218–24.

Padden, C. and Humphries, T. (1988) *Deaf in America. Voices from a Culture*. London: Harvard University Press.

Pickersgill, M. (1998) Bilingualism: Current policy and practice. In S. Gregory, P. Knight, W. McCracken, S. Powers and L. Watson (eds) *Issues in Deaf Education*. London: Fulton Press.

Pickersgill, M. and Gregory, S. (1998) *Sign Bilingualism: A Model*. Leeds: LASER.

Robinson, K. (1991) *Children of Silence*. London: Gollanz.

Sacks, O. (1989) *Seeing Voices*. London: Picador.

Stokoe, W. (1960) *Sign Language Structure*. Silversprings, MD: Linstok Press.

Swanwick, R. (1998) The teaching and learning of literacy within a sign bilingual approach. In S. Gregory, P. Knight, W. McCracken, S. Powers and L. Watson (eds) *Issues in Deaf Education* (pp. 58–68). London: Fulton Press.

Webster, A and Webster, V. (1993) *Supporting Learning Hearing-Impairment*. Avon: Avec Designs.

Woll, B. (1998) Development of signed and spoken languages. In S. Gregory, P. Knight, W. McCracken, S. Powers and L. Watson (eds) *Issues in Deaf Education* (pp. 58–68). London: Fulton Press.

Wood, D., Wood, H., Griffiths, A. and Howarth, I. (1986) *Teaching and Talking with Deaf Children*. Chichester: John Wiley.

Index